Mina's Guide to Minute Taking

Principles, Standards & Practical Tools

Eli Mina

Eli Mina Consulting
Vancouver, BC, Canada

National Library of Canada Cataloguing in Publication:

Mina, Eli, 1949
    - Mina's guide to minute taking: principles, standards, & practical tools / Eli Mina

ISBN 0-9734428-0-8

    1. Corporate minutes. I. Title. II. Title: Guide to Minute Taking.

HF5734.5.M563 2004   651.7'7   C2003-906867-6

Publisher:

Eli Mina Consulting
Vancouver, British Columbia, Canada

Web page: http://www.elimina.com
E-mail: eli@elimina.com
Phone: 604-730-0377

For ordering information visit http://www.elimina.com.

Cover and Inside Design: Louise T. Gallant

Printed in Canada

This guide is not to be construed as legal advice.

Contents

Acknowledgments

I wish to thank my clients and workshop participants, who continually presented me with so many diverse and challenging questions, and helped me develop my expertise in this field.

I wish to give special thanks to the 11 individuals who so graciously offered to serve on my editorial board. You provided valuable insights and feedback and helped make the book meaningful and relevant. My sincere thanks go to:

- Syd Baxter, City Clerk, City of Vancouver, British Columbia
- Rollie Cox, Instructor, Madison Area Technical College, Wisconsin
- Wendy De Marsh, Executive Assistant, School District 57, Prince George
- Rosemary Ishkanian, Registrar, College of Dental Technicians of BC
- Josette A. Lory, Deputy City Clerk, City of Boyne City, Michigan
- Christine Mills, Board Relations Manager, BC's Children's Hospital Foundation
- Wendy Olafson, Executive Assistant, Envision Financial, Langley
- Rae Ratslef, President, Raincoast Ventures – The Minute Taking Professionals
- Brenda Sims, Municipal Clerk, Resort Municipality of Whistler
- Shelley A. Westlake-Brown, Executive Assistant, Real Estate Council of Ontario
- Lorna Wolfe, Executive Assistant, Fraser River Port Authority

I also wish to thank Shelley Harrison Rae for copyediting this book.

Introduction

Minute taking can be complex, tricky and challenging. Minute takers are often expected to produce concise and coherent summaries out of chaotic and disorganized meetings. Many are directed to take minutes without documented guidelines on what to record and what to leave out, and without a prior explanation of issues and technical terms used at a meeting. Sometimes they require a rare combination of diplomacy and fortitude, to deal effectively with demands to record inappropriate details in the minutes.

Minutes of meetings are important documents, for recording consensus and decision-making, and for tracking the evolution of issues and the history of an organization. This book offers principles, standards and practical tools to help reduce anxiety about minute taking and establish clarity on what to record. It also explains how minute takers can build rapport with their groups and generate respect for their work.

Specific questions this book will address:

▶ How much of the discussion should be recorded, and how can arguments about minutes be avoided? Learn to shift the focus of minutes from words to key concepts and ideas, and find out how to convert discussions into concise, coherent and objective summaries.

▶ How much procedural detail should be recorded in minutes of formal meetings? Find out how motions, amendments and other formal procedures should be recorded. Learn which procedural details are significant and which are extraneous.

▶ How much detail should be recorded in minutes of closed meetings? Learn to balance the need for transparency and access to information with the occasional need for confidentiality. Find out how to organize agendas of open and closed meetings, to preserve confidentiality.

▶ Who should tell the minute taker what to record? Learn to formalize a policy on minute taking standards, so the minute taker will take guidance from the group as a whole, and not from individual members.

Some words of caution:

▶ This book will be of limited use if the only person reading it is the minute taker. Although the book is based on sound principles, some of the material may represent significant departures from the practices in many organizations. It would be unrealistic to expect a minute taker to affect changes, single-handedly, to long-established and unproductive practices.

▶ The book will not automatically produce coherent minutes from chaotic and poorly organized meetings. Along with efforts to improve the minutes, there must be efforts to improve the quality of meetings.

▶ Do not be discouraged if this book shows that you have a great deal of work to do to achieve better practices. Instead, build a list of potentially useful ideas and discuss them with all affected parties. Involve them in discussions on which ideas should be implemented immediately and which should be considered for the long term.

▶ This book generally assumes democratic decision-making in meetings. Where this is not the case (for example, in staff meetings, where the manager has the decision-making power), some of the material in this book will not apply.

▶ This book does not constitute legal advice. The author is not a lawyer and cannot advise on what your local statutes require to be included in minutes. In case of doubt or concern about changes to current practices, it may be prudent to consult a legal advisor.

The principles, standards and tools in this book are intended to help you produce clear, concise and useful minutes, and do so with ease and confidence. They can help you make the minute taking task interesting, enjoyable and satisfying.

Chapter

1

Definitions and Key Principles

In this chapter:
- · What minutes are
- · Why minutes are important
- · When minutes are required
- · Who should take minutes
- · Ten key principles for minute taking
- · Ineffective versus effective practices
- · Analysis of poorly recorded minutes

What Minutes are

In a formal sense, minutes are the historical record of an officially convened meeting of an organized decision-making body, such as a board of directors, municipal council, or executive committee. Informally, the term *minutes* can extend to mean a summary of a meeting of a group that is not formally organized, and may or may not have collective decision-making powers. Minutes should generally focus on decisions and actions taken by the group, and may also capture the thought process that led to decisions.

Why Minutes are Important

▶ Minutes enable an organization to meet its obligation to conduct business in a transparent and accountable manner. They keep the organization's membership, stakeholders, or the general public informed on the evolution of decisions that affect them.

▶ Minutes constitute the history of the organization's decision-making processes. Parties who refer to minutes may include the group's voting members (present and future), staff, external stakeholders, the general public, professional advisors, researchers, and others.

▶ Attorneys and the courts may rely on minutes, to assess and judge the validity of actions taken by a decision-making body, and the appropriateness of the procedure used.

▶ Well-organized filing and electronic archiving systems make it possible to use minutes to track past decisions. They can also help prevent repetition of past mistakes or making decisions that conflict with established policies.

▶ Minutes are a follow-up tool. They serve to remind individuals who attended a meeting, and those who missed it, of decisions made and follow-up commitments.

▶ Minutes can help generate the next meeting agenda. For example, issues that were not concluded at a meeting are recorded in the minutes, and then scheduled as *unfinished business* at a subsequent meeting.

When Minutes are Required

Minutes must be taken in official meetings of formally organized decision-making bodies. Types of such meetings include:

▶ Regular meeting (e.g.: monthly board meeting)

▶ Special meeting (dealing with issues that cannot wait until the next regular meeting)

▶ Continued (or *adjourned)* meeting (held to conclude the agenda of another meeting)

▶ Closed meeting (otherwise referred to as an *in-camera meeting* or an *executive session)*

▶ Annual General Meeting (AGM) or Special General Meeting (SGM) of a credit union, public company, or non-profit organization

▶ Teleconference call or videoconference (assuming the legislation, bylaws, or policies of a group permit collective decisions to be made outside face-to-face meetings)

▶ Public hearings sponsored by governments or other publicly accountable bodies

Minutes should also be taken in the following settings (even if not specifically required):

- ▶ Informal staff meetings. Here, minutes are summaries of discussions, consensus, and follow-up actions. Such summaries enable the group to monitor and track progress of initiatives or projects.

- ▶ Planning, teambuilding and problem-solving sessions. Here, minutes are summaries of discussions and consensus. Without concise and complete summaries, the benefits of such sessions and the opportunity for organized follow-up activities are diminished.

- ▶ Negotiations or bargaining sessions. Here, agreements reached should be recorded, but it is not usually necessary to record discussion details.

Minutes are not needed in settings where they are not required and would provide no value. For example:

- ▶ An informal gathering of colleagues
- ▶ An ad-hoc staff meeting for the sole purpose of presenting an update (unless there is a need to inform absent members of what was reported)

Who Should Take Minutes

The minute taker should be chosen with care. The selected individual should have the required skills, and at least a basic knowledge of the group's mandate and issues (see Chapter 7 for tips on boosting the minute taker's knowledge and skills).

Options for choosing the minute taker:

- ▶ The organization may designate a *secretary*, *recording secretary*, *executive assistant*, or *administrative assistant* to take minutes for a group on a regular basis.

- ▶ The individual holding the title of *corporate secretary, executive secretary*, or *secretary-treasurer* may be responsible for the minutes, but usually delegates the minute taking task to a staff member or an outside professional.

- ▶ In closed meetings, where some or all outsiders are excluded, a board or council may designate one of its members to take minutes, or it may delegate the task to a *confidential secretary* (who may be required to sign an oath of confidentiality).

▶ At informal gatherings, the group may designate one of its members to take minutes. In some settings, the group's facilitator takes the minutes, aided by the summaries that he or she articulates from time to time during the meeting.

Ten Key Principles for Minute Taking

1. **Accuracy and completeness:** Minutes should be an accurate and complete record of what took place at a meeting. With the exception of closed (*in-camera*) meetings or very formal meetings, they should cover both the decisions made and the thought process that led to them. Years later, readers should be able to understand what a decision was and why it was made.

   It is inappropriate to alter the minutes before circulating them to the group, except for the sake of accuracy. For example, if a minute taker missed the meaning of a technical point, or did not capture a decision correctly, the group's leader may correct the minutes. However, editing minutes to change an inconvenient decision is not appropriate. Minutes must reflect what actually was done, not what someone wishes had been done.

2. **A focus on key points and decisions:** Except when verbatim (word-for-word) minutes are required for legal or other reasons, minutes should focus on key points and decisions, not on every word said. Individuals rarely express themselves perfectly. Recording their exact words usually provides little or no value and may increase tension and discomfort.

3. **A focus on the business at hand:** Minutes should focus on the business aspects of the meeting and exclude any gossip or extracurricular exchange of information. Simply follow the agenda and record the progress.

4. **A collective focus:** Minutes should focus primarily on the group as a whole, and not on what each individual said or did. Under this principle, minutes would usually not attribute comments to individuals and would not include names of movers and seconders of motions. Individual votes would not be recorded unless, by law or policy, members are entitled to request that their dissent or abstention be recorded, or unless a roll call vote was taken (see Chapter 4).

5. **Objectivity:** Minutes should be free of offensive or inappropriate language, even if such language was used at a meeting. They should not include subjective interpretations of the mood of the meeting or the tone in which comments were made. Phrases like *"There was a heated discussion," "The presentation was very motivational,"* or *"Mr. Davenport was emphatic"* do not belong in minutes. The document should be clean and objective.

6. **Consistency:** Minutes across the same organization should share the same general look and style, and should comply with content and format standards. Such standards should be approved as a policy of the organization (see Chapter 2).

7. **Professionalism:** Minutes should be reviewed thoroughly, and be free of typographical, grammatical or technical errors. A knowledgeable person should proofread technical terms for clarity, before draft minutes are circulated to members.

8. **Readability:** Minutes should be clearly laid out, visually appealing, and easy to read. Long paragraphs should be replaced by concise point-form summaries. Word processing features (bolding, underlining, etc.) should be used to highlight key points and decisions.

9. **A logical flow:** Minutes should be logically organized, even if the meeting itself was fragmented and confusing. If the group addresses an agenda item sporadically throughout the meeting, all events that relate to the same item should be grouped in one place.

10. **Archivability:** Minutes should be easy to archive and retrieve electronically. Standardized names of computer files should be used across the organization. Consistent word strings should be used, wherever possible, for ease of electronic searches. The naming of electronic files should make it easy to link minutes, agendas and reports. The coding of decisions and motions should make it easy to track their history.

Ineffective versus Effective Practices

Category	Ineffective Practice	Effective Practice
Selection of minute taker	Choosing someone with no minute taking skills or no knowledge of the group, its history, issues, or the terminology it uses.	Choosing an individual who has minute taking skills or, alternatively, training them for the job and giving them an orientation on the group and its work.
Treatment of minute taker	Making it unacceptable or unsafe for the minute taker to speak up in meetings.	Making it acceptable for the minute taker to speak up and request clarity.
	Assuming the minute taker is capable of recording coherent minutes in confusing, chaotic meetings.	Conducting clear, well-focused meetings. Taking time to articulate consensus and motions clearly before moving forward.
What is recorded in minutes	A word for word record of who said what.	Concise, readable point-form summaries of discussions and decisions made.
	Using present tense: "The Chair opens the meeting and explains the agenda."	Using past tense: "The Chair opened the meeting and explained the agenda."
	Highlighting decisions made by motions, while not emphasizing decisions made by consensus.	Highlighting motions and consensus-based decisions in the same way.
Expectations and roles	Expecting the minute taker to have shorthand skills or tape the meeting, to capture every word.	Expecting the minute taker to have listening and summary skills, to focus on key points, not every word uttered.
	Allowing the Chair to *doctor* the minutes and change decisions that may be embarrassing to someone.	Allowing the Chair to ensure that minutes are technically and factually clear and accurate.
	Allowing assertive individuals to force the minute taker to record certain comments.	Approving minute taking standards as a formal policy, thereby enabling the minute taker to follow approved standards and not personal wishes.

Analysis of Poorly Recorded Minutes

Below is an excerpt of poorly recorded minutes from a poorly run meeting. It shows why it is important to establish standards for minutes and for meetings.

Text of minutes	Analysis
The November meeting was opened even though some members did not come on time. President Smith said it was very inappropriate to come late. He spoke with passion and members were deeply moved by his opening remarks.	Missing context: the exact date, time, place and group's name. Was a quorum present? Subjective interpretations of the strength of a comment and the response of the members do not belong in minutes.
Mr. Jones moved and Mrs. Humphrey seconded that the minutes be approved, although they are hard to read and contain too much information. Lengthy discussion took place. Mr. Thompson said he was sorry for voting in favor of the motion on the new building and moved to amend the minutes by replacing *Campbell street* by *Maple Street.* The suggestion was greeted with enthusiasm, despite groans by Mrs. Ray.	Members may not change history by amending the minutes. If they want to change an adopted motion, they can do it only after the minutes are approved. Too many subjective remarks and irrelevant information. It is not clear whether the minutes were approved.
Mrs. Jackson insisted that it be recorded in the minutes how fed up she was with committee meetings and that she didn't think our guest speakers amounted to anything.	Minutes should not be a *free for all,* with vocal members dictating what should be recorded. Insulting comments do not belong in the minutes.
Mr. Thompson moved that dinner be served during meetings. Mrs. Jackson seconded, and then moved to insert the word *hot* before *dinner.* The amendment was adopted.	The amendment was adopted, but what happened to the main motion?
At 9 p.m., the meeting was adjourned.	It's about time.

Chapter

2

Minute Taking Standards

In this chapter:
- Benefits of standards
- Standards for recording substantive details
- Standards for recording procedural details
- Standards for the layout of minutes
- Standards for filing and electronic archiving
- Selecting standards
- Formalizing standards
- Creating concise and objective summaries (Sample)

Benefits of Standards

It is highly recommended that you establish minute taking standards for use across the organization. Standards should be established in four main areas:

▶ Standards for recording substantive details

▶ Standards for recording procedural details

▶ Standards for the layout of the minutes

▶ Standards for filing and electronic archiving

Minute taking standards will help accomplish the following results:

▶ Consistency of content and format of minutes across the organization

▶ A tool with which to train new minute takers and orient group members

▶ Establishing an understanding that minutes are significant documents

▶ Reducing arguments about what to record in the minutes

▶ Eliminating demands on minute takers to record inappropriate details

▶ Preserving the integrity of the organization's historical records

▶ Making it easy to retrieve minutes and track the history of motions and decisions

▶ Adding validity to the minutes (because consistent standards are followed, internal and external parties will see minutes as legitimate and genuine historical records)

▶ Reducing exposure to risk that may arise from having inappropriate details in minutes

▶ Creating an organizational incentive to develop standards for planning and running meetings (after all, it is hard to record good minutes in poorly run meetings)

Standards for Recording Substantive Details

Substantive details relate to the actual issues dealt with by the group. They are different from the procedural details, which relate to how decisions were made and how rules of order were used (see next section).

As a minimum, minutes must capture substantive decisions made, and actions taken by the group, at a duly convened meeting. As an option, the group may also include summaries of the discussions and thought processes that led to decisions.

A common dilemma is how much of the substantive discussions to record. Recording too much is problematic in various ways (see further). Recording too little may not give an adequate historical perspective on how decisions were reached.

Substantively, there are three types of minutes:

▶ Decision-only minutes

▶ Anecdotal minutes (decisions and discussion summaries)

▶ Verbatim minutes (word-for-word records of what was said)

Decision-Only Minutes

Decision-only minutes exclude any discussion summaries and capture only what transpired at a meeting: decisions made, and actions authorized. Technically, this is the minimum that common books on rules of order require.

Some boards and councils require *decision-only* minutes for their own meetings, but require anecdotal minutes for committee and staff meetings, and may require verbatim minutes for special speeches, and some public hearings or portions thereof.

Decision-only minutes are the safer standard for closed meetings, (typically dealing with sensitive issues), since recording discussion details may expose the organization to risk (e.g.: if minutes are subpoenaed as evidence by a court of law).

Please note: Although decision-only minutes are shorter (and, in the case of closed meetings, less risky), they offer less historical value than anecdotal minutes.

Anecdotal Minutes

Anecdotal minutes are the recommended standard in most cases (with the possible exceptions of closed meetings and very formal meetings). Anecdotal minutes contain objective and concise point-form summaries of discussions, without attributing comments to individuals. Summaries are followed by decisions made, or motions voted on (if any).

Anecdotal minutes are a compromise between verbatim minutes (see next section) and decision-only minutes. Anecdotal minutes are shorter and less personally focused than verbatim minutes. Conversely, they go beyond recording only decisions and motions, and include *snapshots* (concise summaries) of the thought process that led to decisions. Such summaries are very valuable when researching an organization's history.

To record anecdotal minutes, the minute taker must listen to discussions and capture significant points made by the group. He or she should not record a brief comment, made by one person, and not pursued by the group. On the other hand, the minute taker should record an idea or concern reinforced by several people or given some airtime. A point that was made several times needs only to be recorded once. The minute taker must capture the key concepts or ideas, and not be preoccupied with every word.

To help with the recording of anecdotal minutes, the meeting Chair should periodically summarize key points or record them on a flipchart. Alternatively, the group may allow the minute taker to repeat a summary for confirmation or correction.

For example, the Chair or the minute taker may say, "*Let me sum up the key points you made so far. The key points in favor of this idea are __, __ and __. The two main concerns are __ and __. The consensus is __. The action item is that Jack will check with Management and report at the next meeting. Did I capture it correctly? Is anything missing?*"

The minute taker must never alter summaries according to his or her personal biases. Minutes must be a true and objective reflection of the group's deliberations and actions.

Sample 2.1 at the end of this chapter includes an illustration of how to convert a group's discussion into a concise, objective, organized and useful summary.

Verbatim Minutes

Verbatim minutes are a word-for-word record of *who said what* at a meeting (possibly omitting offensive language, repetitive phrases, broken sentences, and extraneous details).

Use verbatim minutes in exceptional circumstances only, for example:

▶   In some meetings, when the decision-making body considers certain statements or speeches significant enough to record verbatim

▶   In some public hearings, usually at the discretion of the decision-making body

▶   When it is legally required to have a verbatim record of a meeting or a portion of it

▶   When the group considers it prudent to record certain statements verbatim

If your group is accustomed to verbatim minutes, the following arguments may persuade it to accept a change in practice:

▶ Verbatim minutes are lengthy and tedious to read. Members may ignore them. Outside parties may find them confusing and frustrating.

▶ Exceptional skills are required to capture every word at a meeting. A minute taker may require shorthand or court reporting experience. He or she may need to tape the meeting, and may spend considerable time preparing the minutes. Not many people have shorthand or court reporting experience, and it can be expensive to hire those that do. This is neither necessary nor cost effective. The group could put the minute taker's talent to better use.

▶ Verbatim minutes can be embarrassing, when members discover how imperfectly they speak. As a result, arguments may ensue: "*I did not say this,*" "*Yes you did,*" "*But that is not what I meant.*" In addition, it can be frustrating to some members, when the written minutes do not capture vocal inflections and may make them sound harsher than intended. All this discomfort is unnecessary.

▶ Verbatim minutes can preclude natural, free-flowing discussions. Members may hesitate to speak for fear of how their comments will appear in the minutes. A typical concern raised when issues are sensitive is: *Can anything I say at this meeting be used against me in a court of law?* Under such conditions, creativity and spontaneity suffer.

▶ Verbatim minutes focus on individuals, instead of focusing on the decision-making body as a whole. This has the potential to personalize and politicize the group's culture.

▶ Verbatim minutes are a waste of time, paper, and other resources.

▶ Verbatim minutes can place the minute taker in the awkward position of having to decide whether to record offensive language, outright lies, or personal attacks that - in the heat of the moment - could go by unnoticed, but if printed, could prompt affected individuals to initiate action for libel.

Standards for Recording Procedural Details

In addition to standards for recording substantive details, the group should agree on standards for recording procedural details during formal meetings. Meeting procedures include various motions used to facilitate discussions and shared decision-making (see Chapter 4).

It is recommended that insignificant procedural details be removed from minutes of formal meetings, except where they are necessary for clarity and completeness, or where local legislation or bylaws specifically require that they be recorded. For example:

▶ It is not necessary to record names of movers and seconders of motions. The two individuals do not own the motion once debate on it begins. In addition, recording these names may give a potentially false impression that the individuals supported the motion throughout the decision-making process, when this may not have been the case.

▶ If a main motion is amended, it is not necessary to record housekeeping amendments (often-called *friendly amendments*) separately. All that matters is the *final wording* of the main motion and the voting outcome on it. However, an amendment that is significant or divisive should be recorded separately.

▶ If the vote on a motion was clear and conclusive and no one challenged it, there is no need to count or record the number of votes in favor and against the motion or the number of abstentions. The only record needed is of the outcome; i.e.: whether the motion was adopted or defeated.

▶ In large meetings, there is no need to record how each individual voted (unless a roll call vote was taken). All that matters is whether the motion was adopted or defeated. However, in boards or councils, a member can usually request to have his or her dissent or abstention recorded (for more details see Chapter 4).

Standards for the Layout of Minutes

A standardized layout of the minutes provides a consistent look across the organization. Word processing features should be used to make the standard layout readable and visually appealing. Next are a few suggestions.

A Header

A running header, indicating the nature of the document and its status on every page should be considered. Having the same information at the top of every page will ensure that, if pages separate, readers will be able to re-assemble them easily. A running header should indicate the date, the group that held the meeting, whether the minutes are confidential (as is the case for a closed meeting), whether these are approved or unapproved minutes, an archiving reference number, and a page number (if not already included in the footer).

Two examples of headers with sample archiving reference numbers:

| Minutes | ABC Board Closed Meeting 20/6/2004 | Approved 2/7/2004 | Confidential |
| Page 1 of 3 | Archiving Reference MIN-BC-200604 | | |

| Minutes | XYZ Council Regular Meeting 20/1/2005 | Approval Pending |
| Page 2 of 2 | Archiving Reference MIN-CR-200105 | |

Explanation of archiving reference numbers:

MIN-BC-200604: Minutes (MIN) Board (B) Closed Meeting (C) Date (20 June 2004)
MIN-CR-200105: Minutes (MIN) Council (C) Regular Meeting (R) Date (20 January 2005)

A Footer

A footer can be used to show page numbers (if not already included in the header). It can also include information about follow-up activities, or indicate that subsequent revisiting of a decision resulted in a change or reversal.

Please note: Footer notes are solely the recorder's notes, intended to assist readers, and are not considered part of the minutes. Minutes are a record of what took place at the meeting, not what took place after the meeting.

Example of a footer:

Note 1: Funds were forwarded to the Red Cross on April 12, 2007.
Note 2: This motion was rescinded on April 20, 2007. See motion __ (give reference #)

Columns

A column system may make the minutes more readable. For example:

Agenda item (Give title & archiving code for motions)	Concise summary of key points made during the discussion	Decisions made or motions voted on, and whether they were adopted or defeated	Follow-up actions (who will do what and by when)

Other Layout-Related Tips

▶ Establish font styles and sizes (which may be increased when highlighting decisions or motions), desired length of paragraphs (try for no more than five lines each), and how much white space is needed to make minutes readable and visually appealing.

▶ Use word processing features for clear identification of consensus, decisions, action-items and motions. Consider **bolding**, underlining, boxes, etc.

▶ If minutes are long, consider starting with *a table of contents* and *a condensed table of* all decisions, motions and action items. The latter table should include decisions made formally (by motions) as well as decisions made informally (by consensus).

▶ Consider a glossary of terms and abbreviations for minutes of technical meetings, to make it easier for non-technical readers to understand what transpired at the meeting.

▶ Establish writing standards for the entire organization. For example:

  • Minutes reflect the organization's history and should be written in the past tense (*The Board decided to* ___), and not in the present tense (*The Board decides to* ___).

  • Establish whether references to names (where names are recorded) should be formal (Mayor Jones, Ms. Smith), on a first name basis (Jeremy), or by initials (JKH). If it is the latter, include a list of all initials and names at the start of the minutes.

  • Ensure correct spelling, grammar, and punctuation.

▶ Prepare samples of minutes and templates that reflect the above layout standards, share them across the organization, and use them to train new minute takers.

Standards for Filing and Electronic Archiving

Minutes are valuable historical records of the organization and its decision-making processes. It is therefore important to standardize the way they are filed and archived. The goal is to make it easy for internal and external parties to locate minutes, retrieve relevant details, and track the history of issues, decisions and motions.

Printed Minutes

For printed minutes, consider the following tips:

▶ Minutes of meetings of different decision-making bodies should be filed in separate binders. Minutes of board or council meetings should be filed separately from minutes of committee meetings and separately from records of public hearings. Minutes of annual meetings of members or shareholders (non-profit societies, credit unions, or public companies) should be filed in their own separate binder.

▶ Minutes of closed meetings should be filed separately from minutes of open meetings. It is prudent to store binders of closed meeting minutes in a locked cabinet away from public access. This practice enables the group to maintain confidentiality while making non-confidential minutes available for public access (see Chapter 5 for more details).

▶ The minutes in each binder should be organized chronologically, with the most recent minutes available first.

▶ Each set of minutes should have a standardized document reference number, so minutes of a specific meeting are easy to locate. See examples of coding reference numbers given earlier in this chapter, under *headers.*

▶ It may be desirable to assign reference numbers to all reports, significant agenda items and motions. Such numbers should be shown in agendas and minutes. For example:

REP-EC-060405 = Report (REP) Education Committee (EC) dated 6 April 2005

RES-AGM-2006-15 = Resolution (RES) #15, 2006 Annual General Meeting (AGM)

Electronic Archives

If your organization does not currently have electronic archiving of minutes, be forewarned that organizing such a system is likely to be a significant, complex, and labor-intensive undertaking. Nevertheless, if you are taking your organization and its history seriously, such an undertaking is essential. Consider the following tips:

▶ Plan before starting. Think through how your minutes will be used and organize your electronic archiving system accordingly for convenience.

▶ Your ultimate goal should be to have the entire history of your organization accessible electronically. The end result should be that the history of an issue or a motion would be easy to track electronically through searches by reference numbers or word strings.

▶ Establish standards for naming electronic files and directories, and make these standards known to everyone, so they are used consistently across the organization.

▶ Establish standards to facilitate easy searches by key words or concepts. When referring to an issue in the minutes, similar titles and word strings should be used whenever possible, so it is easy to track the history of issues and decisions.

▶ Start by electronically archiving minutes that are already on your organization's computers. Then begin to convert older printed minutes into electronic form. It will be a tedious and lengthy process, so a long-term commitment is needed.

▶ Do not wait to start your new electronic archiving system until you have all the old files in the same electronic form. Move forward now and pick up old files over time. In the interim, consider making old files available electronically by using Adobe pdf files.

▶ If required to make minutes available for public access, post all non-confidential minutes to your organization's web site (after they are approved).

▶ Your electronic archiving system should be user-friendly and allow for easy searches of minutes by non-technical people (such as your membership or the general public).

▶ Always store a current backup of electronic documents at a different location, for the possibility of flood or fire.

▶ You may wish to consult a qualified archivist for advice on electronic archiving and retrieval.

Selecting Standards

Below is an example of a form to consider for selecting minute taking standards. It reflects the standards recommended in this chapter. You may choose to:

▶ Modify the form by choosing options most relevant to your organization.

▶ Vary the standards for different types of meetings. For example: *decision-only minutes* for formal meetings and closed meetings, *anecdotal minutes* otherwise, and *verbatim minutes* in very limited cases, at the discretion of the group.

Category of Standards	Options	Your Selection
Recording substantive details (Discussion and decisions)	Decision-only minutes	Council meetings & closed meetings
	Anecdotal minutes	Committee meetings
	Verbatim minutes	At Council's discretion
Recording procedural details (Format meetings)	Names of movers	Not recorded
	Names of seconders	Not recorded
	Amendments	Housekeeping amendments not recorded separately
	Individual votes	Dissents recorded on request
Layout and flow	Header	Yes (give sample)
	Footer	Yes (give sample)
	Columns	Two (give sample)
	Other layout-related standards	Specify and give sample
Filing and archiving	Code for minutes	Give sample
	Code for significant agenda items	Give sample
	Code for significant motions	Give sample
	Code for reports	Give sample

Formalizing Standards

If your current minute taking practices are not satisfactory, you can use the process below to develop and establish minute taking standards:

▶ Advise your decision makers (Council, Board, Chief Executive Officer) of your intention to develop minute taking standards for their review and approval. Explain the reasons for establishing standards and get their support for the initiative.

▶ Develop a preliminary set of standards addressing the issues raised in this chapter. Mark the document *"Draft for Discussion Purposes."* Include sample minutes reflecting your new ideas, compare them with current minutes, and explain the proposed changes and the reasons for them. Make the explanations clear, objective and compelling.

▶ Engage minute takers and meeting attendees in discussions of the draft standards. Get their feedback, integrate legitimate ideas into the draft standards, and then send everyone an updated copy for final comments. Including everyone in this process will increase the likelihood that they will understand and implement the new standards willingly.

▶ Present the standards to your decision makers. If you require approval by a Council or a Board, prepare a motion such as: *"Resolved that the minute taking standards as proposed be approved."*

▶ Once the standards are approved, minute takers will be able to do their jobs with comfort, clarity and confidence. They will be able to deal effectively with demands to record inappropriate details in minutes. Arguments about what goes in minutes will be minimized.

Sample 2.1:
Creating Concise and Objective Summaries

The next sample shows how to convert a discussion into a concise, objective summary. The left hand column is the conversation, from a fictional mining company's safety committee meeting. The right hand column shows the key facts and concepts captured for the minutes. The summary follows next.

Conversation	Key Points
Chair (Ron): "I called this meeting to try and figure out what happened to our safety procedures that such a terrible accident happened. As you may know, Jack Roberts drove the heavy-duty truck yesterday without wearing a helmet and a seatbelt. He apparently drove too fast and lost control and the truck dropped from the top of the mine pit to the bottom. He is now in hospital with serious injuries. It is very upsetting. We need to analyze what happened and learn from it."	Serious accident No helmet or seat belt Speeding
Charlie: "This happened because everyone is so upset about our contract dispute with the company. It's been dragging on for far too long. We're getting paid so little, and it's hard to blame people for being unhappy and getting sloppy on the job. How can you be happy about work when you can hardly feed your family and pay the bills? Can someone tell me?"	Contract dispute and pay levels may affect morale and safety.
Richard: "And they expect us to read the training manuals to prevent accidents. Did you look at those training manuals? Did you see how outdated they are? Plus they are written in such small print. And I know for sure that several people here can't even read. I'm not sure Jack is literate, and he would never admit it if he wasn't."	Safety manuals outdated. Font too small. Illiteracy may be an issue.
Stephanie: "I think the main problem is the root of all evils: Money. To really have a good safety program, we need money. But our CEO is more interested in money for shareholders, and doesn't realize how stupid this is. Not investing in safety will cost them more in the long run."	Safety versus profits. Long term costs of not investing in safety.
Raymond: "It's all the fault of Jack's supervisor. Why did he let Jack drive the truck without wearing safety gear? And how come we don't have technology on trucks that won't let you start unless you're wearing a seatbelt? Plus we've been talking about speed bumps, so why didn't they put them up? If that's not enough, those helmets are so uncomfortable. Can't they give us something normal human beings can wear without going home with a headache?"	Supervisor's role New technology Speed bumps Helmets uncomfortable.
Chair (Ron): "It won't do us much good to sit here and complain. We have to decide what to tell Management. In the past they didn't pay attention to us because we didn't explain ourselves well. We have a new minute taker. Chris, how can we communicate better to Management?"	Need to focus on solutions and make a credible presentation.

Continued on next page

Chris (minute taker): "Thank you Ron. Let me summarize what I have written for the minutes:

Chair Ron Milner stated the purpose of the meeting: To discuss what led to a recent accident, where an employee was seriously injured when a company truck he was driving crashed, while he was apparently speeding and not wearing safety gear. The Chair suggested that the committee identify the causes of the accident and make suggestions to Management on what can be done to prevent repeat occurrences in the future.

The following main problems were identified:

- The on-going contract dispute and the current pay levels may be having a negative impact on employee morale. This may reduce attention to detail and thereby increase the risk of accidents.
- Training manuals are outdated, the font is too small, and there may be illiterate employees who cannot read them and are too embarrassed to admit it.
- There are questions among some people about Management's commitment to investing in safety. It was questioned whether Management realized that not investing in safety may be costly in the long run.
- Closer supervision might have prevented the employee from driving without wearing safety gear.
- Technological advances might have prevented the employee from starting the truck when not wearing safety gear.
- Speed bumps might have prevented or lessened the impact of the accident.
- Helmets are not comfortable to wear. Improvements should be considered.

Did I record the discussion correctly? Did I miss anything?"

Having identified the problems, the committee will discuss solutions. The remainder of the minutes may be as follows:

In light of the above concerns, the Safety Committee decided to request that Management act as follows:

- Make a concerted effort to resolve the contract dispute soon and treat concerns about pay levels seriously.
- Hire a professional writer to make safety manuals more current and more readable.
- Offer literacy training on a confidential basis and develop alternative means to safety manuals as a means of educating staff about safety.
- Boost the company's commitment to safety, let employees know that safety is job one, and ensure that future communications and actions match these words.
- Explore what can be done by way of better supervision or technological means to prevent employees from driving if they are not wearing safety gear.
- Install the planned speed bumps at the mine as soon as possible.
- Explore what can be done to make helmets more comfortable to wear.

Chapter

3

Minutes of Informal Meetings

In this Chapter:	· Chapter Focus
	· Opening segment
	· Body of the minutes
	· Closing segment
	· Information exchange meetings
	· Problem-solving sessions
	· Approval of significant documents
	· Minutes of an informal meeting (Sample 3.1)

Chapter Focus

This chapter includes guidelines for taking minutes of informal meetings, such as staff meetings, project review meetings, and planning and teambuilding sessions. Groups attending such meetings are not formally organized as decision-making bodies under legislation or bylaws. Participants have no votes, there is no formal quorum requirement, parliamentary procedure is rarely used, and decisions are made by consensus. In such meetings, minutes are usually not a legislated requirement, but are taken for record keeping and follow-up.

Opening Segment

The opening segment of the minutes of an informal meeting should describe the context of the meeting, and include the following details:

▶ Type of meeting

▶ Name of group and organization

▶ Day, date, time and location of meeting

- ▶ Attendance (If the group is large, a list of attendees is usually not needed)
- ▶ The name of the meeting chair
- ▶ The name of the minute taker

For the sake of clarity, it may also be helpful to record:

- ▶ The overall purpose of the meeting
- ▶ A list of the main agenda items

Sample Opening Segment

Minutes of Monthly Meeting
Information Systems (IS) Department, ABC Company

Date:	Wednesday July 16, 2003
Place:	Headquarters Meeting Room 1
Time:	8:30 a.m.
Chair:	Rachel James
Attending:	Derek Ng, Jack Robson, Ruth Smith, Joanne Jameson (taking minutes)
Absent:	Rob Thornton
Guests:	Tina Ford, IS Specialist, Price Waterhouse
Meeting purpose:	To consider payroll system improvement options
Agenda items:	Opening remarks Consultant's presentation and discussion Decision on system improvement options

A few tips for the opening segment:

- ▶ In most meetings, there is no need to record which members arrived late or departed early, unless there is some significance to these facts.

- ▶ It is not usually necessary to distinguish between absent members who gave advance notice that they would miss the meeting (*regrets),* and those who were absent without notice.

- ▶ Some of the information in the opening segment can be included in a running header, at the top of every page in the minutes. For example:

Minutes   ABC Company Information Systems Department Monthly Meeting   16/7/2003
Page 1 of 3   Archiving Reference #: _____

Body of the Minutes

The body of the minutes of an informal meeting should include concise summaries of discussions and decisions made on various agenda items. It is important to highlight the group's *consensus* or *decisions* and draw special attention to *action items* agreed to. (See specific examples in further sections in this chapter.)

Closing Segment

The closing segment of the minutes of an informal meeting should include:

▶ Optionally, a consolidated table of action items (grouping items in one place, for follow-up purposes). Some groups prefer to have such a table in the opening segment of the minutes, while others prefer to have it as an extra document, separate from the minutes.

▶ Date of the next meeting

▶ Closing (or adjournment) time

Sample Closing Segment

Recap of action items (Optional)

Agenda item	Action items	Individuals responsible
1. Customer complaints	Call Bernice Smith about her complaint	Ron Stewart
2. Staff training	Call ABC Trainers for clarifications	Judy Johnson

Next meeting: Tuesday August 12, 2003, 8:30 a.m.
 (Location to be arranged)

The meeting was closed (or adjourned) at 9:50 a.m.

Information Exchange Meetings

Staff teams usually meet on a regular basis for the purpose of giving and receiving updates on progress. The information exchange should be summarized in concise point form.

A few tips for recording information exchange sessions:

▶ Review any pre-circulated reports and create a concise point-form summary of the main ideas before the meeting. This portion of the minutes can be completed before the meeting begins.

▶ Avoid entering the text of an entire report in the minutes. Capture key points only, and give the reference by which the full report can be located, for example, REP-PC-030512, which is the report (REP) of the Personnel Committee (PC) dated 03 May 2012.

▶ If a member had nothing to report, it is not necessary to record this fact. However, if an item was on the agenda and was not addressed, the record should reflect something like: *"The Education Committee did not present a report."* Every agenda item should have a corresponding entry in the minutes.

Sample Minutes of an Information Exchange (excerpt)

Agenda item 2: Manager's report

Manager Rebecca Dean reported the following main points:
- (Record key ideas and concepts)

In response to questions, Rebecca made the following clarifications:
- (List follows)

Agenda item 3: Progress reports

Sean Roberts reported the following main points:
- (List follows)

Problem-Solving Sessions

In a problem solving session, the group may have a free flowing discussion, pausing periodically to summarize progress and establish consensus. The logical progression of problem solving is as follows (see sample minutes below):

▶ Identifying the problem

▶ Establishing criteria that any solution should meet

▶ Brainstorming for solutions

▶ Evaluating the solutions

▶ Choosing the best solution

In reality, your members may not necessarily progress in such an organized manner. Nevertheless, you can still organize the minutes to reflect a logical thought process.

Sample Minutes of a Problem-Solving Session

Team members participated in a problem-solving session regarding office space issues. A summary of the discussion is as follows:

Team members identified the following problems with the existing office space:

- Uneven distribution of office space
- A few tight and potentially unsafe spots around the office
- Unnatural flow from one working area to another
- Inefficient placement of workstations
- Separation of members of the same team from one another

The team agreed that any solutions to the problem would have to:

- Provide a smooth flow between working areas.
- Prevent hazards and maximize safety.
- Help build cohesive teams.
- Be more comfortable than the current configuration.
- Fit within the department's budget.

The team brainstormed for solutions and narrowed the focus to the following options:

- Take immediate actions to address safety concerns.
- Create an office space committee with representation from all departments.
- Engage an interior design firm to redesign the office space.
- Look for new premises.
- Accept the current situation as imperfect but workable.

The team evaluated the above options and decided to:

- Reject the option of accepting the current situation.
- Begin to address safety concerns (Ron Fox to pursue with Management).
- Investigate the cost of design services (Rick Hyde to obtain quotes).

Approval of Significant Documents

A group may hold a meeting to discuss and approve an important or complex document, such as a proposed negotiation strategy or a significant and contentious new policy. An effective facilitator and a good recorder are essential to the success of such a meeting.

Sample Minutes: Approval of a Negotiation Strategy

Consultant Ken Chow presented the document "Towards a Healthy and Successful Community" (Reference# _____). Ken indicated he had prepared the report in consultation with the Chief and Council, and some members of XYZ First Nation.

Ken emphasized the following key points:

- (Key points summarized)

Discussion ensued. Several housekeeping changes to the document were approved by consensus. The members also made the following substantive changes:

- Page 1: 2nd paragraph, changed from 5 years to 10 years.
- Page 5: 3rd paragraph, added the sentence: The members of the community will be advised on progress monthly and will be consulted on any significant new initiatives.

Overall, the following main points were made in the discussion:

- It was agreed that it was important to have a negotiating strategy, to help clarify issues to government agencies with which the Chief and Council will negotiate.
- It was agreed that it was important to proceed expeditiously with the negotiations, so short and long-term needs of the community can be met.

Members approved the modified document. They then directed the Chief and Council to develop plans consistent with the principles and values outlined in the report.

Sample 3.1: Minutes of an Informal Meeting

Minutes of Monthly Meeting
Human Resources (HR) Committee of XYZ Company

Date:	January 15, 2005
Time:	2:00 p.m.
Place:	Committee room 5
Attending:	Derek Lee, Human Resources Department (Chair)
	Theresa Green, Accounting Department (Recorder)
	Monica Rothberg, Information Technology Department
	Fred Ferguson, Customer Service Department
Absent:	Rebecca Stein, Marketing Department
Agenda:	1. Staff recognition program
	2. Internet access policy

Agenda item	Discussion, Consensus & Action items
1. Staff Recognition	Derek indicated that the committee had been asked to develop guidelines for staff recognition. He suggested that two key topics be addressed: • Types of achievements and performance that should be recognized • Methods of staff recognition
Consensus	After discussion, the Committee agreed to recommend the following: • In the preliminary stages, recognition should be given for excellent customer service and high productivity. • Recognition should be non-monetary (such as the employee of the month award) and monetary (such as bonuses based on performance).
Action items	The following action items were agreed to: • Derek will prepare a report and present to Management. • Committee members will present additional ideas at the next meeting.
2. Internet Access	Monica reported on research she had done on policies of similar companies on Internet access during working hours. She suggested the policy cover these issues: • Whether employees should be allowed to send and receive private e-mails at work • Whether employees should be allowed to browse the Internet at work
Consensus	It was agreed that the Committee should recommend a policy stating that internet access for private use be allowed only during lunch breaks.
Action item	Monica and Derek will prepare a draft policy for discussion at the next Committee meeting.
Next meeting	February 17, 2005, 2:00 to 4:30 p.m. Committee Room 5.
Adjournment	4:15 p.m.

Chapter

4

Minutes of Formal Meetings

Chapter Focus

This chapter provides guidelines for recording minutes of formal meetings, including meetings of boards, councils or committees, and general meetings of members or shareholders of an organization. In such meetings, typically:

▶ The group is formally constituted as a decision-making body.

▶ The group is usually governed by legislation and bylaws.

▶ Members have voting powers.

▶ A quorum must be present to make valid collective decisions.

▶ Parliamentary procedure (rules of order) may be used.

▶ It is legally required to record minutes of meetings.

Opening Segment

The opening segment of the minutes of a formal meeting should describe the context of the meeting. Specific details to be recorded are:

▶ Meeting type: Regular, Special, Closed (*In-Camera or Executive Session*), Continued (*Adjourned*), or Annual

▶ Name of group, Board, Council, Committee, General Membership, Shareholders, etc.

▶ Name of organization

▶ Day, date and location of the meeting (an actual address may be needed)

▶ Attendance: For a board, council or committee, record the names of those who attended and those who were absent. For a large meeting (such as an annual meeting of members or shareholders), record only the number of members who were present, and show whether the quorum requirement was met. An actual list of attendees should not be required in this case, but such a list may be included as a separate file.

▶ Name and title of the meeting Chair

▶ Name and title of the minute taker

▶ Time the meeting was called to order

Some of the above information can also be included in a running header that appears at the top of every page of the minutes.

A few tips on recording attendance:

▶ It is not usually necessary to record the names of individuals that arrived late or departed early. An exception is if the total number of members present is very close to a quorum. In this case, the minutes should show whether a quorum of the group was present when voting took place. Decisions made in the absence of a quorum are technically invalid.

▶ Some organizations record names of members who were absent during certain votes. While this is not usually required, it may be prudent to do so in a political setting.

▶ If a member declares a conflict of interest and leaves the meeting, the minutes should show the member's declaration and indicate that he or she was absent from the meeting while the group discussed and voted on the issue (see separate section in this chapter).

▶ It is not usually necessary to distinguish between members who gave notice of their absence (*regrets)* and those who did not (*absent without notice*), except in the case where an extended absence from meetings may warrant suspension or dismissal.

Sample Opening Segment

Minutes of the Regular Meeting of the Aberdeen Scotland City Council

Date:	Monday, August 25, 2003
Place:	Council Chambers, 3333 Kings Road, Aberdeen, Scotland
Presiding Officer:	Lord Mayor Rachel James
Councilors present:	Councilors Jacob Berge, Jacqueline Roberts, etc.
Councilors absent:	Councilor Ron Stewart

A quorum was present throughout the meeting.

Staff in attendance:	Joan Kerri, City Manager
Ron Dobson, City Clerk
Brian Smith, Legal Counsel
Robert Pickering, Executive Assistant (minute taker)

Lord Mayor James called the meeting to order at 7:05 p.m.

Sample Running Headers

For unapproved minutes:
Minutes   Regular Council Meeting   25/8/2003   Approval pending
Page 1 of 4   Archiving reference # _____

For approved minutes:
Minutes   Regular Council Meeting   25/8/2003   Approved 17/9/03
Page 1 of 4   Archiving reference # _____

Body of the Minutes

The body of the minutes of a formal meeting should include motions, proce-dures, and voting outcomes (see further sections).

A few points to note:

▶ The group should choose either decision-only minutes (recording only mo-tions and actions) or anecdotal minutes (adding concise summaries of dis-cussions), and avoid using verbatim (word for word) minutes. See Chapter 2 for details.

▶ Decisions made informally (by unanimous consent) have the same validity as those made formally (by motions), and should be equally highlighted. Further sections in this chapter describe how to record both informal and formal decision-making.

▶ This chapter assumes the group opts not to record names of movers and seconders in minutes (see further section for explanation). If this is not the case in your organization, you will need to convert all given samples from "*It was moved and seconded*" to "*It was moved by ___ and seconded by ___.*"

Closing Segment

The closing segment of the minutes of a formal meeting includes:

▶ The date of the next meeting (if set)
▶ The closing time (adjournment)

Sample Closing Segment

The Mayor advised Council that the next Regular Council Meeting was scheduled for Monday September 8, 2003 at 7 p.m. at Council Chambers.

The meeting was adjourned at 9:50 p.m.

If adjournment was by a motion, record it as follows: *"It was moved and seconded that the meeting be adjourned. The motion was adopted and the meeting was adjourned at 9:50 p.m."*

Informal Decisions (Unanimous Consent)

Routine and non-controversial decisions do not require formal motions. They may be made by unanimous consent. The Chair asks, *"Is there any objection to ___?"* If there is no objection, the Chair then directs that the action be taken. The principle is: if there is no objection, there is acquiescence and therefore unanimous consent. However, if there is even one objection, the Chair resorts to a more formal procedure and may need to take a formal vote on the matter.

Unanimous consent is not appropriate when voting on main motions or resolutions, nor is it appropriate for any contentious procedural decisions. In such instances, formal motions and formal votes may be required to allow for differences of opinion (see further sections).

Below are two examples of recording decisions made by unanimous consent. See subsequent sections for more examples of recording unanimous consent.

What transpired	Minutes
An unscheduled delegation requested permission to address the Municipal Council. Mayor: "Is there any objection to allowing the delegation from the Red Cross to speak to Council for 5 minutes? (Pause) There being no objection, Ms. Roche, you have the floor for 5 minutes."	By unanimous consent, Council allowed a delegation from the Red Cross to address Council for 5 minutes.
Adjournment: Chair: "Is there any further business? (Pause) If not, the meeting now stands adjourned."	There being no further business, the meeting was adjourned at 10:15 p.m. Or, more simply: The meeting was adjourned at 10:15 p.m.

Housekeeping Items

In the course of a formal meeting, the following housekeeping items may be addressed:

▶ Approval of the agenda

▶ Approval of meeting rules

▶ Approval of minutes

▶ Handling reports and correspondence

▶ Handling a consent agenda

Approval of the Agenda

What transpired	Minutes
Informal process (Unanimous consent)	The following changes were made to the agenda: • Added discussion of financing options (item 7.2) • Changed the sequence by moving the discussion of new premises (item 6) before item 3 The agenda as amended was then approved
Formal process (A motion)	It was moved and seconded that the agenda of the Rosedale Club regular board meeting of February 22, 2004 be approved. The following changes were made: • Change A • Change B The motion as amended was adopted.

Approval of Meeting Rules

If a group meets infrequently (e.g.: annually), it is prudent to formally adopt a few rules at the start of the meeting. Such rules may include a speaking protocol (such as raising hands in a small meeting or speaking from a microphone in a large meeting). Rules may also include speaking limits (such as speaking up to two times on a motion, no longer than three minutes each time, with second-time speakers giving way to first-time speakers).

What transpired	Minutes
Informal process (Unanimous consent)	The following meeting rules were approved by unanimous consent: (A bulleted list of rules follows).
Formal process (A motion)	It was moved and seconded that the rules shown in the document entitled Meeting Rules of the Annual Shareholders Meeting of ABC Company held on April 15, 2007 be approved. An amendment to increase the speaking time limit from two minutes to three minutes was adopted. The motion as amended was adopted.

Approval of Minutes

What transpired	Minutes
Informal process (Unanimous consent)	The minutes of the April 22, 2002 regular meeting of the Board of the Lakeville Co-op were approved. Or, if corrections were made: The minutes of the April 22, 2002 regular meeting of the Board of the Lakeville Co-op were approved with the following corrections: (a list of corrections follows)
Formal process (A motion)	It was moved and seconded that the minutes of the April 22, 2002 regular meeting of the Board of the Lakeville Co-op be approved. The motion was adopted. Or, if corrections were made: It was moved and seconded that the minutes of the April 22, 2002 regular meeting of the Board of the Lakeville Co-op be approved. The following corrections were made: _____. With these corrections, the motion was adopted.

Handling Reports and Correspondence

What transpired	Minutes
A report was presented orally (without written backup), for information only. The group does not require motions to receive reports after they are presented.	Tom Rothberg, Education Committee Chair, reported the following: (A bulleted list is given.)
There was a printed report and the presenter discussed key points. No recommendations were presented for approval. Since a written backup is available, there is no need to re-enter the entire report in the minutes. Only the key points highlighted at the meeting may need to be included.	Rebecca Jones, Chair of the Business Development Committee, presented a report entitled Strategic Partnerships 2000 (REP-BDC-191004). Key points discussed with the Board were: • (A bulleted list is given.)
Same example, but the group follows the practice of having motions to receive reports after they are presented (It should be noted that a motion to receive a report after it was presented is usually meaningless and has no real impact. It is also unclear what happens if the motion to receive is defeated).	Same start as above It was moved and seconded that the report of the Business Development Committee (REP-BDC-191004) be received. The motion was adopted.
A letter from a citizen requested the board to reject a rezoning application. The board has the practice of adopting motions to receive letters after presentation (Here again the motion to receive has no real impact).	A letter from Ms. Joan Roper expressing opposition to rezoning bylaw RZ-151202 was presented. It was moved and seconded that the letter be received. The motion was adopted.
A report was presented and contained a recommended motion.	The Finance Committee presented its report, including a recommendation of a 15% member dues increase. It was moved and seconded that the Board of Directors of the Garden Club of St. Louis increase member dues by 15%. The motion was defeated.

Handling a Consent Agenda

To free up time for substantive issues, all housekeeping items and non-contentious decisions can be grouped under a *consent agenda*. Any member may request that an item be removed from the consent agenda for separate consideration. Only one motion is needed to adopt all items remaining on the consent agenda.

What transpired	Minutes
No item was removed from the consent agenda and it was approved as a package by one motion.	It was moved and seconded that the consent agenda of the May 15, 2005 Regular Meeting of the Board of Newcastle Growers' Co-op be approved, including the following items: • Approval of meeting agenda • Approval of minutes of April 24, 2005 regular Board meeting • A motion to receive all reports listed on the agenda • A motion to approve expenses listed in the Treasurer's report The motion to approve the consent agenda was adopted.
One item was removed from the consent agenda and treated separately.	The consent agenda was presented. The following item was removed from the consent agenda: • Approval of the minutes of the May 7, 2005 Special Meeting of the Board It was moved and seconded that the items remaining on the consent agenda of the May 15, 2005 Regular Meeting of the Board of Newcastle Growers' Co-op be approved, including the following items: (Bulleted list given; excluding the item that was removed). The motion was adopted. It was then moved and seconded that the minutes of the May 7, 2005 Special Meeting of the Board of Newcastle Growers' Co-op, which were removed from the consent agenda for separate consideration, be approved. The following corrections were made: _____. With these corrections, the motion was adopted.

Formal Decisions (Motions)

A motion is a formal proposal that the decision-making body take certain action.

Various types of motions are covered in this chapter:

1. Main motion (or resolution): a proposal that the group take substantive action (e.g.: make a purchase) or formally adopt an advocacy position (e.g.: officially endorse or oppose another organization's policy on a given issue)

2. Amendment: a motion to modify the wording of another motion before voting on it

3. Motions to avoid or delay a vote on a main motion that is being debated

4. Motions to revisit previous decisions

5. Procedural motions: motions to address procedural issues, e.g.: a point of order, a motion to close debate, etc.

Notices of Motion

Many public bodies require any new main motion to be preceded by a *notice of motion*, so members can consider it before debate begins. Under this practice, a member states his or her intention to propose a main motion at the next meeting. The notice of motion is recorded in the minutes (*"Director Smith gave notice of his intention to propose a motion to _____ at the next Board meeting"*) and the main motion itself is placed on the next meeting agenda.

Phrasing a Main Motion

The minute taker may be in position to help phrase main motions. Consider these tips:

▶ A main motion should be clear, concise, unambiguous and complete. It should include a full context, making it possible to pull the motion out of the minutes as a stand-alone excerpt. Instead of *"It was moved and seconded that the Board authorize a $550 donation to the Salvation Army"*, record: *"It was moved and seconded that the Board of Directors of Make a Wish Foundation of Ontario approve a donation of $550 to the Salvation Army."*

▶ Lengthy main motions should be submitted in writing, in advance of any discussion. It is good practice to include main motions in the pre-meeting package. This will enable the minute taker to paste pre-written main motions into an agenda-based computer template.

▶ Motions that conflict with the group's legislation, bylaws or policies, are not allowed and should be declared out of order.

Phrasing a Resolution

A resolution is an elaborately phrased main motion. A resolution may open with a series of *Whereas* clauses, which state the reasons for a proposed action. This series is followed by *Resolved* clauses, which state the actions to be taken (see sample below).

The minute taker may be requested to help phrase resolutions. Consider these tips:

▶ The number of *Whereas* clauses should be minimized. Too many of them dilute the *Resolved* clauses. It is technically acceptable not to have any *Whereas* clauses.

▶ *Whereas* clauses should be based on facts, not on opinions or advocacy positions.

▶ *Resolved* clauses should be capable of standing on their own, regardless of what the *Whereas* clauses say. For example: "*Resolved, That the above situation be addressed*" is inadequate, even if *the above situation* was explained in the *Whereas* clauses.

Here is an example of recording a resolution:

It was moved and seconded that the following resolution be adopted:

Whereas, There has been an increasing number of incidents of property crime against businesses in downtown Hopeville;

Whereas, Such incidents appear to have had negative impacts on businesses in the downtown core and could potentially become an impediment to new businesses establishing themselves in this area; and

Whereas, The Council of the City of Hopeville believes the downtown core has a lot to offer to residents and tourists alike, and that it is in the City's best interests to support local businesses and attract new ones to the downtown core; now therefore be it

Resolved, That City staff be directed to assure merchants in the downtown core that the Council of the City of Hopeville shares their concerns about the increased frequency of crime, and that City Staff be directed to solicit merchants' ideas on what can be done to reduce crime; and

Resolved, That the Police Chief be directed to advise the Council of the City of Hopeville by July 31, 2008 of methods and resources required to reduce property crime in the downtown core.

The resolution was adopted.

Moving and Seconding a Motion

Moving and seconding are procedural steps that formalize the introduction of motions. The significance of these steps is often overplayed. Closer attention must be given to the precise wording of the motion, the debate, and the voting outcome. It should be noted that, under parliamentary procedure, it is not absolutely essential to have motions moved and seconded, and they may also be assumed by the chair. For example, the Chair may say: "*The Finance Committee report includes the following motion: ___. The Chair will assume the motion and open it for debate. Is there any discussion on this motion?*"

Many organizations follow the practice of recording names of movers and seconders in the minutes. There are several arguments against this practice:

▸ It shifts the focus of the minutes from the group's collective actions to the actions of individuals. This can politicize and personalize the decision making process. Some individuals may move or second motions for personal credit only.

▸ It may give a potentially false impression that the mover and seconder supported the motion, when this may not have been the case. The mover, after hearing the debate, may be persuaded to vote against the motion. The person seconding a motion may be doing so only for the purpose of opening it for discussion. She or he may even be opposed to the motion and hope that the group will formally defeat it.

▸ It gives a false impression that the motion belongs to the mover and seconder in perpetuity. Some people even believe a motion cannot be revisited at a later meeting if the mover and seconder are not present. In fact, once debate begins, ownership and control of the motion shifts to the group, and the mover and seconder no longer have unilateral control over it.

▸ Members may feel intimidated to move and second unpopular motions. There is a story about a homeowners association where movers and seconders of contentious motions found their cars vandalized as soon as the minutes were published.

Options to consider:

▸ If your group is not explicitly required to record names of movers and seconders, it should adopt a policy of not recording such names in the minutes. This does not mean that motions will not be moved and seconded, but only that the names will not be recorded. Under this approach, the minutes will read as follows:

"It was moved and seconded that the Board of the XYZ Credit Union commission a study on public attitudes towards financial institutions. The motion was defeated."

▶ Alternatively, if your group chooses to record names of movers and seconders, minutes will read as follows: "It was moved by Director Jackson and seconded by Director Rupert that the Board of the XYZ Credit Union commission a study on public attitudes towards financial institutions. The motion was defeated."

The samples in the remainder of this chapter omit names of movers and seconders. Adjust these samples if your group opts to continue recording those names in the minutes.

Screening a Motion

The Chair is not automatically required to open a motion that was moved and seconded for debate. The Chair may refuse to recognize a motion that conflicts with the group's legislation, bylaws or policies. The Chair may also request that the wording of a motion be clarified, or that it be presented in writing before debate begins.

If the Chair screens a motion, your record will be as follows:

What transpired	Minutes
The Chair declared that a motion was out of order.	It was moved and seconded that the Board of the XYZ Credit Union be instructed to change the lending policy and stop discounting loans to staff.
	The Chair ruled the motion was out of order, as the Credit Union Rules gave the Board exclusive jurisdiction over the lending policy. He indicated, however, that the Board would take this suggestion under advisement.
The Chair requested that the motion be submitted in writing	There is usually no need to record such requests in the minutes. Just record the actual wording of the motion.

Debating a Motion

The amount of debate recorded in the minutes depends on the standard adopted by the group. (See Chapter 2 for details).

Three examples of recorded debate:

Adopted Standard	Recording the debate
Decision-only minutes (No debate recorded)	It was moved and seconded that the Board of Education of Beaver County approve the proposed policy on equal access to libraries. The motion was adopted.
Anecdotal minutes (A concise summary of the debate is recorded, without attribution of comments to individual members.)	It was moved and seconded that the Board of the Freedom of Information Society of Alabama lobby the State Legislature to reduce restrictions on access to information. The main points made in favor of the motion were: • (Point form summary, recording each distinct point only once) The main concerns raised about the motion were: • (Point form summary) The motion was defeated.
Verbatim minutes (A word-for-word record of the debate)	Word for word minutes (possibly removing inappropriate language and off–topic comments, eliminating repetitive phrases, and completing broken sentences) With very few exceptions, verbatim minutes are not recommended (see Chapter 2).

Voting on a Motion

In most instances, voting outcomes are clear and there is no need to count the votes. In such cases, the Chair declares the outcome and moves on. The minutes simply state:

"The motion was adopted." or
"The motion was defeated."

However, if the outcome is close, votes should be counted, and the minutes should show the number of votes in favor and against the motion. For example:

"The motion was adopted by a vote of five in favor to three against."

A tie vote usually means that the motion was defeated. Some groups expect the Chair to vote only to break a tie, but this practice is problematic, and should only apply if your legislation or bylaws require it. For example: if the vote is five in favor and four against, the Chair – if a voting member - should be able to vote against, create a tie, and cause a defeat of the motion. Before imposing any restrictions on the Chair, check your legislation, bylaws, and selected book on rules of order for any applicable provisions.

Unanimity is not usually a requirement for adopting a motion, but some groups like to record whether a vote was unanimous or not. In most cases, unanimity means that no one voted against the motion, even though some members may have abstained (see below). Some bylaws define unanimity as having every member present voting in favor.

Abstentions: The meaning of an abstention depends on your legislation or bylaws. Suppose there are four votes in favor of a motion, three against, and four abstentions:

▶ If the legislation or bylaws are silent on how to interpret abstentions, they are not counted, in which case the motion would be adopted by a vote of four in favor to three against.

▶ Some statutes or bylaws stipulate that an abstention is counted as a vote in favor, in which case the above motion would be adopted by a vote of eight in favor to three against.

▶ Some statutes or bylaws stipulate or imply that an abstention is counted as a negative vote. In this case, the motion would be defeated by a vote of four in favor to seven against.

Majority and super-majority: Most motions require a majority vote to be adopted (a majority, sometimes referred to as a *simple majority,* means more votes are cast in favor of a motion than against it). However, your legislation or bylaws may specify that certain motions require a super-majority, such as a 2/3 or 3/4 vote, for adoption.

Individual Votes

Under the principles of collective decision-making and collective accountability, only the collective outcome is significant, not how each individual voted. Recording how each individual voted on a motion is generally not required.

Exceptions to this general guideline are as follows:

▶ In boards or councils, it is customary to accommodate individual requests to record a dissent or an abstention (see previous section on how to interpret abstentions). Some organizations go further by allowing members to have their reasons for dissenting or abstaining recorded in the minutes. This practice is not recommended, because it shifts the focus substantially away from the group as a whole and towards individuals.

▶ The legislation or bylaws of some public bodies require the recording of all negative votes. Others stipulate that all votes (positive and negative) must be recorded on demand.

▶ The legislation or bylaws of some public bodies allow a member who was absent from a meeting to record his or her dissent on a decision that was made. Such recorded expressions of dissent are not actual votes, and do not affect the outcome (assuming the decision was validly made in a meeting at which a quorum was present).

▶ Under parliamentary procedure, the group may order (by a majority vote) that the vote be taken by roll call. In this case, each member is polled and his or her vote is recorded.

Note: There is a significant difficulty with mandating that individual votes be recorded. It is often not clear whether such a requirement applies only to main motions, or to amendments and procedural votes as well. If your organization's legislation is not specific on this issue, the group may wish to adopt a bylaw article saying: "*Unless ordered otherwise by the Board in specific cases, recorded individual votes shall only apply in the case of main motions.*"

Examples of recording individual votes

The Situation	Minutes
There is a legislated requirement to record all negative votes.	The motion was adopted. Councilors X, Y, and Z voted against the motion.
There is a requirement to record all votes.	The motion was defeated. The vote was as follows: • In favor of the motion: Councilors A, B, C • Against the motion: Councilors D, E, F, G, H • Abstentions : Councilors I, J
A roll call vote was ordered.	*A roll call vote was ordered, and the vote was as follows:* • Councilor A Yes • Councilor B No • Councilor C Abstain • Councilor D Yes • Councilor E Yes • Mayor Jones Yes *The motion was adopted by a vote of four in favor, one against, and one abstention.*

Conflicts of Interest

Conflict of interest policies are intended to protect the integrity of a group's decision-making processes, by excluding individuals whose judgment may be impaired by a potential personal benefit from a decision to be made by the group.

A member who has a conflict of interest should act as follows:

▶ Declare the conflict at a meeting, before the discussion of the issue commences

- Leave the meeting and remain absent until the issue has been concluded (so he or she does not inhibit the discussion by being present at the meeting)
- Avoid influencing members' opinions on the issue at the meeting or away from it

The minutes should show the member's declaration and the fact that he or she was absent for the duration of the discussion and the vote on the issue at hand. Including such a statement in the minutes protects both the individual member and the organization.

Example of recording a conflict of interest in the minutes:

Agenda item 8: Awarding cleaning contract

Councilor X stated that he had a conflict of interest on this issue because his wife, who owns a cleaning company, was bidding on the contract. He left the meeting after making the declaration and was called back after the vote on the motion was taken.

Amending a Motion

Members may propose amendments while a main motion is being debated. An amendment is a proposal to change the wording of a motion by adding, inserting, deleting, or replacing text. Under standard parliamentary procedure, there can be only one primary amendment (an amendment to the motion) and one secondary amendment (an amendment to the amendment) pending at the same time. An amendment must be closely related to the central subject of the motion, but does not have to support the intent of the motion.

The suggested approach for recording amendments is as follows:

- For a housekeeping or *friendly amendment* (i.e.: a non-controversial change) there is no need to record it separately. The final wording of the motion is all that is necessary.
- For a substantive or contentious amendment, the group may want to record it separately, even if your parliamentary book suggests recording only the final wording of the motion.

What transpired	Minutes
Friendly amendments (non-contentious changes, usually approved informally, by unanimous consent)	A motion relating to the purchase of computers was moved and seconded. After debate and housekeeping amendments, the following motion was adopted: "That the Board of the Brookhills School authorize the purchase of 3 Toshiba laptop computers, at a total cost not exceeding $5000, including all taxes and delivery costs."

Contentious amendments:
 	
The amendments are indented for better readability.
 	
Note: Under some books on rules of order, there is no need to record amendments separately, even if they are contentious. If this practice is followed, the minutes will be as follows:
 	
"A motion relating to an awards event was moved and seconded. After debate and amendment the following motion was adopted: (final wording follows)."
	It was moved and seconded that the Greeley Garden Club hold an awards reception on June 22, 2003.
	
	    It was moved and seconded to amend the motion by adding the words 'with spouses included.'
	
	        It was moved and seconded to amend the amendment by inserting the words 'or significant others' between 'spouses' and 'included.'
	
	        The amendment to the amendment was adopted
	
	    The amendment to the main motion was adopted.
	
	The main motion as amended was adopted, with the final wording being as follows:
	
	That the Greeley Garden Club hold an awards reception on June 22, 2003, with spouses or significant others included.
	
	(See note on the left column).

Delaying or Avoiding a Vote

There are times when a group prefers to delay or avoid a direct vote on a main motion. While the main motion is on the floor, it is in order for a member to:

▸ Move to postpone consideration of the main motion to a certain time

▸ Move to refer the motion to staff or a committee for analysis

▸ Move to table the motion

▸ Request that the motion be withdrawn

Each of the above options requires a majority vote to adopt, but an informal agreement, by unanimous consent, is acceptable:

"Is there any objection to postponing consideration of this motion until the next meeting?" Pause. *"There being no objection, the motion is postponed."*

In the following examples, assume the text is preceded by: *"It was moved and seconded that the Motown Apartment Owners Association permit owners and renters to have pets in their apartments, provided that the Association's noise regulations are adhered to."*

What transpired	Minutes
Postponement (By a motion)	It was moved and seconded that consideration of the main motion be postponed until the April 2, 2004 meeting. The motion to postpone was adopted.
Postponement (By unanimous consent)	By unanimous consent, consideration of the main motion was postponed until the April 2, 2004 meeting.
Referral	It was moved and seconded that the main motion be amended by adding the words 'as of January 1, 2005.' It was moved and seconded that the main motion and the amendment be referred to the Rules Committee for advice, with instruction to report back at the April 2, 2004 meeting with answers to the following questions: _____. The motion to refer was adopted.
Tabling	It was moved and seconded to table the main motion, so the Board could hear from the visiting Federal Minister of Housing. The motion to table was adopted, and the Federal Minister of Housing was invited to speak to the Board. Upon the visitor's departure, consideration of the main motion was resumed.
Withdrawal **Note:** If a main motion is withdrawn shortly after it was introduced, there is no need to record it. For example: if new information is given a few minutes after a main motion is moved and seconded, making it clear that the main motion is redundant, and it is withdrawn, there is no need to record it or the fact that it was withdrawn.	*By unanimous consent, it was decided to have the motion withdrawn.* Or, if there was no unanimous consent: The mover requested permission to withdraw the main motion. By a vote of 20 in favor to two against the main motion was withdrawn. (See note on the left hand column)

Revisiting Previous Motions

A decision-making body has the prerogative of revisiting motions and changing its mind.

Below are examples of how to record the revisiting of motions. The details given in footers are for information only. They are not an official part of the minutes, since minutes are a record of what took place at a meeting, and not what took place at a later meeting.

What transpired	Minutes
Revisiting a main motion at the same meeting.	It was moved and seconded that the staff of the Lakeview Community Association be instructed to organize a community workshop on public speaking on March 15, 2007.
Note: Typically, the procedure to revisit a motion at the same meeting is by moving to reconsider the vote. Some books on rules of order and some bylaws allow only those who voted on the winning side to move reconsideration, i.e.: a member who voted in favor may move to reconsider an adopted motion. A member who voted against may move to reconsider a defeated motion.	The motion was defeated.
	Later in the meeting, it was moved and seconded that the vote on the above motion be reconsidered. The motion to reconsider was adopted and debate on the community workshop motion resumed. Additional information was given (concise summary given in the minutes).
	The motion was amended to read as follows: "That the staff of the Lakeview Community Association be instructed to organize a community workshop on listening skills on March 23, 2007". The motion was then adopted.
	Note: For reader-friendliness, it is a good idea to record the revisiting process following the original decision, even if it occurred much later at the same meeting.
Rescinding an adopted motion at a subsequent meeting.	**Minutes of March 15, 2007 meeting (excerpt)** It was moved and seconded that the Boulder City Dog Club hold an awards banquet on July 17, 2007. The motion was adopted (see note 1).
Note: At a subsequent meeting, the motion to rescind is used to cancel an adopted motion. The motion to reconsider is not used, unless the legislation or bylaws allow it.	**Footer on the same page** Note 1: This motion was rescinded at the April 20, 2007 meeting.
The motion to rescind is out of order if the original motion was fully implemented and it is impossible to rescind it.	**Minutes of April 20, 2007 meeting (excerpt)** It was moved and seconded that the motion that the Boulder City Dog Club hold an awards banquet on July 17, 2007, adopted at the March 15, 2007 meeting, be rescinded. The motion to rescind was adopted.

Continued next page

Amending an adopted motion at a subsequent meeting.

Same notes under Rescinding (previous example) apply.

Minutes of March 15, 2007 meeting (excerpt)
It was moved and seconded that the Boulder City Dog Club hold an awards banquet on July 17, 2007. The motion was adopted (see note 1).

Footer on the same page
Note 1: This motion was amended at the April 20, 2007 meeting by replacing the word 'banquet' with 'reception', and by changing the date from July 17 to July 25, 2007.

Minutes of April 20, 2007 meeting (excerpt)
It was moved and seconded that the motion that the Boulder City Dog Club hold an awards banquet on July 17, 2007, adopted at the March 15, 2007 meeting, be amended by replacing the word 'banquet' with 'reception' and by changing the date from July 17 to July 25, 2007. The motion to amend was adopted.

Reintroducing a defeated motion at a subsequent meeting.

The appropriate procedure to revisit a defeated motion at a subsequent meeting is to re-introduce and record it as new business.

Procedural Motions

The table below shows how to record typical procedural motions not already covered earlier in this chapter. The motions are listed in alphabetic order. If your group uses motions that are not covered here, you can apply similar principles to record them.

Procedural Motion	Minutes
Appeal Members disagreed with a Chair's ruling.	The Chair's ruling that the amendment was not in order was appealed. The ruling was upheld by a vote of seven in favor to four against.
Closing debate (also known as *Calling the Question* or *Moving the Previous Question*)	It was moved and seconded that debate be closed. The motion was adopted by a vote of fifteen in favor to three against.
Consider informally This procedure allows informal discussion of an issue without a motion on the floor.	It was moved and seconded that the topic of environmental management be considered informally for 30 minutes. The motion was adopted.
Division of the assembly Members who doubt the voting outcome can request a standing vote.	Division was called and the Chair directed that the vote be counted. The count was 35 in favor and 42 against. The main motion was defeated.

Division of the question
A motion can be divided in order to consider specific parts separately.

By unanimous consent the main motion was divided, and parts 1 to 3 were considered separately from part 4.

Parts 1-3 of the motion were adopted.

Part 4 was referred to the Finance Committee for analysis, with instruction to report to the Board at the March 22, 2004 regular meeting.

Note: The actual minutes should show what each part was.

Parliamentary inquiry
Used to make a procedural inquiry

A member inquired as to when it would be in order to move an amendment to the main motion. The Chair advised that this could be done once the current amendment was voted on.

Note: It should not be necessary to record in the minutes every parliamentary inquiry and the response to it.

Point of information
A request for information

After the presentation of the audited financial statements, the auditor addressed the following questions by members: (list of inquiries and answers follows)

Point of order
Used to point to a perceived violation of a law, bylaw, rules of order, or policies

A member raised a point of order that the Chair was not allowed to speak in debate. The Chair ruled that the point of order was not well taken, since the rules did permit the Chair to speak in board meetings, provided the Chair joined the speakers' lineup and did not dominate the discussion.

Question of privilege
Used to complain about noise, heat, or other matters relating to the comfort of the group

Often the issue at the core of the complaint is addressed quickly and there is no need to record it in the minutes.

Ratify
Used to confirm and validate action taken outside a legal meeting or without a quorum

It was moved and seconded that the Board of the ABC Club ratify the actions taken at the May 22, 2004 meeting, where a quorum was not present. The motion to ratify was adopted.

Schedule a continued meeting
Also referred to as scheduling an *adjourned meeting*. A *continued meeting* is a meeting to conclude the agenda of another meeting.

It was moved and seconded and adopted that the Board of Truro County schedule a continuation of the meeting on October 20, 2006 at 6:00 p.m. The remaining items to be covered were: _____ .

The meeting was then adjourned at 10:15 p.m.

Suspend the rules
A motion to suspend a procedural rule to enable the group to accommodate an unusual circumstance.

Minor rule suspensions should not be recorded. For example, if the rules were suspended to allow a member to speak for four minutes instead of three, this information offers no value. However, it may he useful to record that:

By unanimous consent, it was agreed to suspend the rules and replace the pending main motion and all amendments with the following main motion: _____

Nominations and Elections

If nominations and elections are conducted at a meeting (and not by mail ballot), they should be recorded as follows:

Nominations

The following nominations were made:

For President:	Ruth Cheng (Nominated by the Nominating Committee)
	John Cruise (Nominated from the floor)
	Troy Lindsay (Nominated from the floor)
For Vice President:	Jim Smith (Nominated by the Nominating Committee)
	Ron Lampson (Nominated from the floor)
	Caroline Foy (Nominated from the floor)

(Continue with other positions).

Election results
The election was by ballot and the results were as follows:

Office of President

Total ballots cast:	547
Number of spoiled ballots:	3
Votes necessary for election:	274
Ruth Cheng received	150 votes
John Cruise received	279 votes
Troy Lindsay received	115 votes

John Cruise was elected President.
(Continue in a similar manner with other positions)

It was moved and seconded that the ballots be destroyed 30 days after the adjournment of the meeting. The motion was adopted.

Notes:

▶ The above example assumes that a majority of all ballots (including spoiled ballots) is required to elect a person to an office. Your bylaws or rules of order may have a different requirement, such as a majority of all legal ballots (excluding spoiled ballots).

▶ Some organizations prefer not to record the number of votes received by each person, for fear of embarrassing low vote getters. This practice is potentially problematic, since no proof of actual election results will be available once ballots are destroyed. Unless the bylaws state otherwise, the actual numbers should be a part of the official record.

Sample 4.1: Minutes of a Formal Meeting

Minutes of the Regular Meeting of the Council of the City of Rockfort

Place:	Council Chambers
Date:	Monday, November 3, 2003
Attending:	Ron Stewart, Mayor (presiding) Councilors Jane Smallwood, Richard Jones, Thomas Richardson
Absent:	Councilor Ruth Smith
Staff:	Alice Wood, Municipal Administrator Ken Thompson, City Clerk Ron Dobson, Administrative Assistant (taking minutes)
Call to order:	7:00 p.m.

Agenda item	Discussion and Decisions
1. Consent agenda (1.A to 1.C, and 1.E)	It was moved and seconded that the items on the consent agenda, except item 1.D. (below) be approved: 1.A. The agenda for the meeting 1.B. A special rule to allow public delegations to speak for 3 minutes each 1.C. Approval of the minutes of the October 20, 2003 regular meeting 1.E. A motion to authorize staff to respond to all recent correspondence The motion was adopted.
1.D. Minutes of the October 27, 2003 special meeting	It was moved and seconded that the minutes of the special council meeting of October 27, 2003, which were removed from the consent agenda, be approved. The motion was adopted after the following corrections were made: (A bulleted list of corrections follows).
2. Bylaw xyz123: Re-zoning from residential to commercial	It was moved and seconded that Council give Bylaw xyz123 first and second reading. The motion was adopted. It was then moved and seconded that Council schedule a public hearing on the proposed re-zoning on November 18, 2003, starting at 7 p.m. The motion was adopted. The Mayor instructed staff to choose the location and advertise the public hearing as required by the legislation.
3. Grant application by Rockfort Arts Council	A delegation representing Rockfort Arts Council presented an application for funding in the amount of $10,000. It was moved and seconded that the above application be approved. It was then moved and seconded that the amount be reduced from $10,000 to $7,500. The amendment was adopted, and the main motion as amended was then adopted as follows: "That the Council of the City of Rockfort approve funding in the amount of $7500 for the Rockfort Arts Council."

Continued next page

4. Policing

It was moved and seconded that the following resolution be adopted: *"Resolved, That Council instruct the City of Rockfort Police Chief to increase police patrols in the Beaumont neighborhood."*

Questions were raised about the financial impacts of this proposal. It was then moved and seconded *that the motion be referred to the City Administrator and the Police Chief for analysis, with an instruction to report back to Council at the regular meeting on November 17, 2003.* The motion to refer was adopted.

The Mayor advised that, in accordance with the approved schedule of meetings, the next regular meeting of the Council of the City of Rockfort would be held on November 17, 2003, starting at 7:00 p.m.

The meeting was adjourned at 9:45 p.m.

Chapter

5

Minutes of Closed Meetings

In this chapter:
· When closed meetings are appropriate
· Who takes minutes of closed meetings
· What to record in minutes of closed meetings
· Preserving confidentiality
· Declassifying minutes of closed meetings
· Organizing agendas of closed meetings

When Closed Meetings are Appropriate

Decision making bodies may meet in closed meetings to discuss confidential matters. Closed meetings are often referred to as in-camera meetings or executive sessions. The term in-camera is derived from Latin and means in closed chambers.

Attendees of closed meetings may include:

▶ Voting members of the group

▶ Individuals mandated or allowed to attend by legislation, bylaws or policy

▶ A confidential secretary to take minutes

▶ Individuals that the group invites to attend, e.g.: legal counsel, etc. Some groups require outsiders to sign an oath of confidentiality before being allowed to attend a closed meeting.

Confidentiality is usually intended to achieve one or more of the following goals:

▶ Protection of the organization, its operations, economic interests, and delivery of its mandate, against possible harm that could result from the release of certain information

- Protection of individuals against an unreasonable invasion of their personal privacy
- Protection of the business interests of third parties

Several topic areas require confidentiality. Any documents relative to such topics (including meeting minutes) are kept confidential. The legislation, bylaws, and policies of an organization may specify particular areas of confidentiality. Typical examples of such topic areas include:

- The security of the property of the organization
- Financial information that, if made public, may be beneficial to the competition or detrimental to the organization itself
- Intimate, personal, or financial details with respect to an individual
- Acquisition or disposition of property
- Decisions with respect to employee negotiations
- Decisions with respect to hiring, termination or disciplining an employee
- Litigation affecting the organization

Many decision-making bodies are subject to Freedom of Information (FOI) and Protection of Privacy (POP) legislation. Such legislation usually specifies what can be classified as confidential, and how the decision to do so is made. Governing bodies must respect such provisions and avoid conducting too much business behind closed doors. There must be legitimate reasons for classifying a matter as confidential, and avoiding embarrassment for office holders is not one of them. FOI legislation may enable citizens to challenge the validity of concealing certain documents, and if successful, gain access to them.

Some organizations follow the practice of holding confidential debates behind closed doors, but finalizing the decisions in open meetings. This practice is problematic, since the group's ability to fully debate any related motions in an open session is likely to be curtailed. Therefore, this practice should be avoided (unless it is mandated by legislation). The group should hold both the debate and the decision-making behind closed doors, to ensure full protection of organizational interests and personal privacy.

Who Takes Minutes of Closed Meetings

Minutes of closed meetings may be taken by:

▶ One of the voting members

▶ A confidential secretary

▶ Another designated person

If the minute taker is an outsider, it is good practice to have him or her sign an oath of confidentiality before the meeting. It is also prudent to confirm verbally that the person fully understands the need to maintain confidentiality.

What to Record in Minutes of Closed Meetings

Given the sensitivity of the issues typically discussed in closed meetings, minutes should include only the minimum information needed to record the decision making process.

A few guidelines:

▶ The main focus of the minutes should be on decisions made by the group. Comments should not be attributed to individuals. Verbatim minutes should be avoided.

▶ Discussion summaries should not be recorded if the organization could be exposed to risk, as in the case of minutes being subpoenaed before a court of law. Specifically, discussion summaries of human resource-related decisions (hiring, firing, discipline, etc.) should be omitted. If there is any doubt about what to record, consult legal counsel about risk management.

▶ If discussion summaries are recorded at all (for historical value) they should be kept to a minimum, in concise point-form, avoiding the identification of *who said what*.

▶ Please note: Removing discussion summaries from minutes of closed meetings leaves a gap in the organization's historical records. This price may need to be paid in the interests of reducing exposure to risk.

Preserving Confidentiality

Tips on preserving the confidentiality of closed meeting minutes:

▶ Do not include confidential items on the agenda of an open meeting. Each agenda item should be assessed before the meeting. If an agenda item is deemed confidential, schedule it on a closed meeting agenda (see further section on organizing meeting agendas).

▶ Unless your legislation or bylaws stipulate otherwise, both the discussion and the decisions on confidential matters should take place in closed meetings. Having the discussion in a closed meeting and the decision at a subsequent open meeting is potentially problematic.

▶ Schedule the approval of closed meeting minutes on agendas of subsequent closed meetings and not on agendas of open meetings. If this is not done, the minutes of the closed meeting become a part of the public record, and this can prove risky.

▶ All confidential minutes, (both draft minutes and approved minutes) should be stamped *confidential* on every page, or display the word *confidential* prominently on a running header.

▶ An option to consider is color-coding of all confidential documents (agendas, minutes and reports), to help distinguish them from non-confidential documents.

▶ Printed confidential minutes should be filed in separate folders or binders under the custody of a confidential secretary. Access to such files should be limited to those who are entitled to see confidential documents. Such files should be kept locked in a secure cabinet, with limited access, away from public minutes.

▶ In some cases, it may be prudent to ask for the return of all copies of closed meeting agendas and minutes, to ensure confidentiality.

▶ If on-line archives of minutes of closed meetings are maintained, use password protection and other security measures to limit access to them.

Regardless of efforts to keep minutes confidential, members sometimes leak confidential information to the public or the press. Such leaks are potentially damaging, and some statutes and bylaws provide for disciplinary measures against members who breach confidentiality.

Consider the following tips:

- ▶ Members should be informed about when and why confidentiality is needed and the risks encountered when confidential documents are leaked, i.e.: The organization's interests may be threatened and the personal privacy of individuals or third parties may be invaded.

- ▶ The group should establish a written policy on confidentiality, along with a formal commitment by members not to leak confidential documents. Some organizations require members to sign an oath of confidentiality before taking office. Penalties for breaches of confidentiality may need to be established.

- ▶ Items that are not justifiably confidential should not be scheduled on agendas of closed meetings. Trying to avoid embarrassment is not by itself a legitimate reason to classify an issue as confidential. Doing this when there is no organizational interest or personal privacy to protect will likely build resentment. This, in turn, may cause some members to challenge the validity of the process by leaking confidential documents. In addition, if your organization is subject to Freedom of Information (FOI) legislation, citizens may apply for access to documents they believe should be in the public domain.

Declassifying Minutes of Closed Meetings

As soon as it becomes clear that the organization's interests or the privacy of an individual or third party will not be compromised by the release of confidential minutes or portions thereof, the decision-making body can vote to declassify the minutes or appropriate portions.

The vote on declassifying confidential minutes should be taken during a closed meeting, in order to allow members to discuss whether the protection of organizational interests or personal privacy is still needed. The motion presented may be as follows:

"Resolved, That the minutes of the closed meeting of the Ferndale City Council held on April 10, 2006 be declassified from confidential to non-confidential."

or:

"Resolved, That the portion of the minutes of the closed meeting of the Ferndale City Council held on April 10, 2006 relating to the topic of labor negotiations (agenda item 6) be declassified from confidential to non-confidential."

After the minutes are declassified, there are two options on how to proceed:

▶ The header can be edited by replacing the word *"confidential"* by *"declassi-fied on (date)"*. The declassified minutes are then filed together with other publicly available minutes.

▶ Alternatively, the Chair can announce all declassified decisions and motions at the next open meeting, thereby making them part of the publicly available record. Under this arrangement, editing or re-filing the original minutes may not be needed.

Organizing Agendas of Closed Meetings

Some boards and councils follow the practice of mixing confidential and non-confidential matters on the same meeting agenda. Non-members are asked to leave when a confidential issue is discussed, and invited back once the issue has been dealt with.

The above practice is disruptive and tends to fragment the meeting. Non-members are put in an awkward position, not knowing how long they'll need to wait. It can also be confusing to take minutes of such meetings and record confidential items separately.

The preferred alternative is to prepare two separate meeting agendas: An open meeting agenda and a closed meeting agenda. The progression on the day of the meetings is as follows:

1. The open meeting is called to order.
2. The open meeting agenda is dealt with.
3. The open meeting is adjourned.
4. Non-members are asked to leave.
5. The closed meeting is called to order (possibly after a short break).
6. The closed meeting agenda is dealt with.
7. The closed meeting is adjourned.

Legislation may require your group to go through a formal process when scheduling an item on a closed meeting agenda. For example: The group may be required to adopt a motion at an open meeting to schedule an item on a closed meeting agenda. Such a requirement makes the scheduling process formal, public and transparent, reducing the likelihood of placing an item on a closed meeting agenda without a legitimate reason for it.

Chapter

6

Approval Process

In this chapter: · Who approves minutes
· Pre-approval activities
· Approving the minutes
· Recording the approval process
· Post-approval activities
· Minimizing errors in the minutes

Who Approves Minutes

Approving the minutes means confirming that they accurately reflect what took place at a previous meeting.

In democratic settings, voting members share decision-making powers and ac-countability. Therefore, in such settings, the group that held the meeting ap-proves the minutes, typically at a subsequent meeting.

The following guidelines apply to who approves the minutes:

▶   In most cases, the group that held the meeting should approve its own minutes i.e.: A board should approve board minutes. A committee should approve committee minutes.

▶   It is a mistake for a committee to bring its minutes to a governing board for approval, since board members did not attend the committee meeting and cannot verify that the minutes are accurate.   It is also incorrect to assume, that if a board mistakenly approves committee minutes, it automatically en-dorses the committee's recommendations.

▶ Annual meetings of societies, credit unions, or public companies are an exception. In such cases, it makes no sense to approve the minutes a year later, since it is unlikely that members will recall what took place at the meeting. In such cases, approval of the minutes should be delegated to the board of directors or a minutes approval committee, which would likely meet shortly after the annual meeting.

▶ To establish the above practice, the following resolution can be adopted at the next annual general meeting of your society, credit union or public company:

"Resolved, That the Board of Directors of the XYZ Credit Union be authorized to approve the minutes of General Meetings as of this 2005 Annual General Meeting, provided that copies of approved minutes be made available to members (or shareholders) on request."

Pre-Approval Activities

A common subject of debate is whether to allow the group's Chair, or any member, to edit the minutes before they are formally presented for approval. Consider these tips:

▶ Editing by the Chair, or anyone else, should only be done for the purpose of technical clarification and accuracy. It is risky to edit minutes to clarify intent, especially if that intent was expressed in a meeting open to the public or outside parties. It is better to ensure the intent is clearly articulated at the meeting. The Chair should slow down and repeat any consensus or motions for clarification, before finalizing any decision or taking any vote. The moment of voting should be treated as a *sacred moment* and must not be rushed.

▶ If a decision was made at a meeting but another decision was actually implemented, the minutes should show the decision that was made. The minutes of a subsequent meeting should include an explanation of why it was necessary to depart from the original decision.

▶ Ultimately, regardless of any *editing* by the Chair or anyone else, it is up to the group to decide whether the minutes are accurate. If the group believes the minutes do not accurately reflect what took place, it should not hesitate to amend them.

Another question to consider is when to circulate draft minutes to members:

▶ If draft minutes are circulated shortly after the meeting, members will be more likely to remember what took place, and better able to help in creating accurate minutes. Members will also be reminded in a timely manner of any follow up duties they agreed to perform.

▶ On the other hand, if draft minutes are circulated to members closer to the next meeting (e.g.: together with the meeting package), members will be better able to use them to prepare for the meeting.

A workable compromise is to send the draft minutes to members by electronic mail shortly after the meeting for feedback. A printed copy of the next draft should then be included with the next meeting package.

Approving the Minutes

The minutes can be approved, either by a motion or by unanimous consent, usually at the next scheduled meeting of the group.

Approval by a Motion

If a motion to approve the minutes is made and seconded, the Chair says: *"It is moved and seconded that the minutes of the February 15, 2001 Regular Meeting of the Board be approved. Are there any corrections to the minutes?"*

A typical mistake is to ask, *"Is there any discussion?"* This can lead the group to spend time repeating debates already concluded at the last meeting. The approval process is only intended to ensure accuracy, not to find out if everyone is comfortable with decisions made at the last meeting. The appropriate question is *"Are there any corrections?"*

Corrections to the minutes, if any, are usually approved by unanimous consent. In this case, the Chair asks, *"Is there any objection to making this correction?"* *pauses*, and then says: *"There being no objection, the correction is made. Are there any other corrections?"*

When no more corrections are forthcoming, the Chair takes a vote: "*The question is on the motion to approve the minutes of the February 15, 2001 Regular Meeting of the Board. Those in favor of this motion raise your hands. Thank you. Those opposed, raise your hands. Thank you. The motion is adopted.*"

It is poor practice to follow the approval of the minutes by asking: "*Is there any business arising from the minutes?*" Asking about *business arising from the minutes* can lead the group to *re-discussing* decisions made at the previous meeting. A preferred approach is to replace "*business arising from the minutes*" with reports on any follow-up items (under *Reports*) and by scheduling any unfinished items under *Unfinished Business*. There should be nothing else *arising from the minutes*.

Approval by Unanimous Consent

Unless the group is required to have motions on every decision, the approval of the minutes can be de-formalized by using unanimous consent. The Chair can say: "*The minutes of the Regular Board meeting held on February 15, 2001 were circulated. Are there any corrections? (Pause) There being no corrections, the minutes are approved as circulated.*"

Any corrections presented should be handled in a similar manner as shown for approval by a motion. When no more corrections are forthcoming, the Chair says, "*There being no further corrections, the minutes are approved as corrected.*"

Disputed Corrections

If there is a dispute about a proposed correction to the minutes, and there is no independent verification of what took place, the Chair can pursue a formal process: "*There is a disagreement on the correction and we will take a show of hands. Those who believe the correction is legitimate raise your hands. Thank you. Those opposed to the correction raise your hands. Thank you. The correction will be made.*"

Additional tips

▶ Some books on rules of order require the Secretary to read the minutes aloud before they are approved. In most cases, such a practice is unnecessary, especially if the minutes were circulated to the members before the meeting. The group can approve a rule to supersede its parliamentary manual and not have the pre-circulated minutes read aloud.

▶ To save time, the vote to approve the minutes can be added to the *consent agenda*, together with other non-controversial items (see Chapter 4).

▶ If the minutes of the previous meeting are not available, this should be noted in the current minutes: "*The minutes of the November 12, 2004 special meeting were not available, and approval was postponed to the January 10, 2005 regular meeting.*" At the next meeting there would be two sets of minutes to approve, in chronological order (older minutes first). The approval of both sets of minutes can be added to the *consent agenda*.

▶ A common but unfounded belief is that no action can be taken on a decision or motion until the minutes are approved. In fact, a decision or a motion takes effect immediately upon its adoption and can be implemented then, unless the motion itself specifies a later date on which it will take effect or be acted upon.

▶ It is not appropriate to change a previous decision or motion by amending the minutes. If a previous decision or motion needs to be changed, this can be done after the minutes are approved (usually by the motion "to amend something previously adopted"). Minutes are a historical record of what was done, not what the group may wish had been done.

▶ A frequently asked question is whether a person who did not attend the previous meeting is entitled to move or second the approval of the minutes, propose corrections to them, or vote on the approval motion. The answer is yes on all counts. A member does not lose the right to participate or vote on any issue, including the approval of the minutes, due to being absent from the last meeting.

Recording the Approval Process

The approval of the minutes should be recorded as shown in the table below.

If a motion was used	It was moved and seconded that the minutes of the April 22, 2002 Regular Meeting of the Board of the Lakeville Co-op be approved. The motion was adopted.
	Or, if changes were made:
	It was moved and seconded that the minutes of the April 22, 2002 Regular Meeting of the Board of the Lakeville Co-op be approved. The following changes to the minutes were made: _____. The motion was then adopted.
If unanimous consent was used	By unanimous consent, the minutes of the April 22, 2002 Regular Meeting of the Board of the Lakeville Co-op were approved.
	Or, if circulated minutes were corrected:
	By unanimous consent, the minutes of the April 22, 2002 Regular Meeting of the Board of the Lakeville Co-op were approved with the following corrections: _____.

Post-Approval Activities

Once the minutes are approved, the following actions should be taken:

▶   The minute taker should make any corrections on the computer file of the unapproved minutes and change the notation on the running header from "*unapproved*" or "*draft*" to "*approved on ___ (date).*"

▶   There is no need to distribute the officially approved minutes to all members. Instead, members can update their own copies of the pre-circulated draft minutes based on the corrections, which are recorded in the minutes of the current meeting.

▶   Approved minutes should be filed in the *Approved Minutes* binder or folder and archived on the computer system, for electronic access, as a *read only* file. Consistency in numbering, filing, and use of key words, will allow for easy historical searches of minutes.

▶   It is customary in some organizations to have printed copies of approved minutes signed by the Corporate Secretary (or equivalent position) and possibly also by the Chair.

▶ There should be separate binders or folders for minutes of different decision-making bodies. Minutes of board meetings should be filed separately from minutes of committee meetings. Minutes of general membership or shareholder meetings should be filed separately from minutes of board meetings.

▶ If minutes are to be available for public inspection, they should be kept in an accessible location. If they are to be distributed, they should be sent as soon as possible after the meeting, and a distribution list should be kept.

▶ There should be separate binders or folders for minutes of closed meetings. These folders must be classified *confidential* and be under the custody of a designated individual, such as a confidential secretary. They should be placed in a locked cabinet, with limited access, away from publicly accessible minutes.

▶ If minutes of closed meetings are archived on the computer for remote access by voting members, they must be password protected and subject to other security measures, to prevent unauthorized access (for more on confidential minutes, see Chapter 5).

Minimizing Errors in the Minutes

Taking time during a meeting to make minor corrections to minutes can be annoying. Every effort must be made to record the minutes as accurately and as professionally as possible.

There are two types of errors to watch for:

▶ Housekeeping: spelling errors, poor grammar, and incorrect technical terminology

▶ Substantive: incorrectly recorded decisions, motions, or discussion summaries

Minimizing Housekeeping Errors

▶ Minutes should be run through a spellchecker and grammar checker and changes made where needed. Please note: the spellchecker and grammar checker are not always right, since spelling may be different from country to country. In addition, a misspelled word may not trigger the spellchecker. For example: both united and untied are correct words.

- The minutes must be reviewed thoroughly and carefully several times, to eliminate awkward sentences or spelling mistakes, and ensure that the document reads well.

- The minute taker should learn the technical terminology used by the group and not hope that members will capture errors in terminology. Silence does not mean agreement that the minutes are correct. Errors that no one caught can be embarrassing or even risky.

- During the meeting, it should be acceptable for the minute taker to ask about the meaning of a technical term or abbreviation. Alternatively, questions can be addressed to the Chair or knowledgeable members after the meeting.

Minimizing Substantive Errors

- The minute taker must listen carefully to the discussion and stay focused.

- The Chair should routinely confirm the consensus or repeat motions before moving on.

- Alternatively, the minute taker can offer to repeat the consensus or motion as understood, for accuracy, before the group moves on.

- It may be useful to tape the Chair's summaries, noting relevant tape counter positions, for subsequent reference.

- Whenever possible, motions should be prepared in advance of a meeting and included in the package sent to members.

- It can be suggested to the Chair or the group that motions or resolutions be in written form before they are considered and recorded in the minutes.

- Members should be provided with sample motions and resolutions to consider as they prepare their own. The minute taker should be available to help members frame any motions prior to the meeting.

- If members end up voting on an unclear motion, trusting the minute taker to interpret what they meant, it may be prudent to delay any action on the motion until the minutes are approved, especially if the motion is contentious or has broad impacts.

Chapter

7

Minute Taker's Checklists

In this chapter:	· Building knowledge and skills
	· Building rapport with the group
	· Preparing for a meeting
	· Pre-meeting activities
	· Activities at a meeting
	· Post-meeting activities
	· Sample 7.1: Meeting agenda
	· Sample 7.2: Minute taking template
	· Sample 7.3: Minute taker's interventions

Building Knowledge and Skills

Taking minutes can be intimidating without the required skills or without any knowledge of the group and its work. Here are some tips on building knowledge and skills:

▶ Before starting to work with the group, the minute taker should ask the Chair, or members, for an orientation on the group's work. The minute taker should also take time to review relevant documents, such as:

• The group's mandate, mission and vision, core values, and strategic plan

• Applicable legislation, especially portions that relate to minutes, access to information, protection of privacy, conflict of interest, and meeting procedures

- The organization's constitution, bylaws, code of ethics, and policy manual
- The group's applicable parliamentary manual (e.g.: Robert's Rules of Order Newly Revised, the Standard Code of Parliamentary Procedure by Alice Sturgis, etc.)
- Minutes and agendas of previous meetings
- Reports and technical documents related to the group's work

▶ The minute taker should continually develop knowledge and skills through courses and conferences of professional organizations, and by inviting feedback and advice from colleagues. Skills to be developed include:

- Business and technical writing
- Active listening, articulation and summary skills
- Speaking to groups
- Time and priority management
- Meeting agenda design
- Crafting motions, resolutions and amendments
- Parliamentary procedure (rules of order)
- Being an effective advisor (combining diplomacy, clarity and honesty)
- Chairing a meeting (in order to assist an inexperienced Chair, if needed)
- Electronic archiving and retrieval
- Word processing and use of spreadsheets

▶ A minute taker may be asked to take minutes for a new group with little or no notice. To reduce anxiety and prepare for such a possibility, the minute taker should learn about the entire organization, become familiar with the mandate of each department and committee, and get to know the particular technical terminology.

▶ A minute taker may benefit from having a personal mentor and coach, usually someone he or she respects and is comfortable confiding in.

Building Rapport with the Group

The minute taker should continually work to build rapport with the Chair and the members of the group. The minute taker can achieve this goal by producing high quality minutes reliably and consistently, anticipating and responding proactively to the group's needs, and being available for help between and during meetings.

In informal settings, it should be acceptable for the minute taker to interact freely with group members between meetings. It should also be acceptable for the minute taker to speak up during meetings and ask for help when needed, e.g.: request that a motion be clarified, ask whether one item should be concluded before moving on to the next, etc.

In more formal settings, the minute taker's interaction may be primarily with the Chair. The minute taker should meet the Chair periodically to discuss their individual roles, mutual expectations, and how best to work together. In such discussions, the minute taker can do the following:

▶ Request feedback from the Chair on what is working well and what should change.

▶ State what is needed in order to produce high quality minutes (a good agenda, clear motions, etc.), and how the Chair can be supportive during and after the meeting. For example: slowing down to articulate summaries, consensus and motions, or reviewing draft minutes after the meeting for substantive and technical accuracy.

▶ Agree on where the minute taker should sit during meetings (ideally close to the Chair, to alert him or her to a problem or request help, quietly and expeditiously).

▶ Agree on the most appropriate way to alert the Chair to a problem during a meeting. Options include: speaking up, passing a note to the Chair, or showing a pre-made cue card (*repeat the motion, take a vote, etc.*).

▶ Discuss how the Chair and the group can make the best use of the minute taker's skills. For example: relying on the minute taker to help with agenda design, crafting motions or resolutions, providing advice on parliamentary procedure, etc.

Preparing for a Meeting

Before each meeting, the minute taker should:

▶ Review meeting documents and become familiar with the issues at hand.

▶ Speak to technical presenters and clarify any new terms and abbreviations. If possible, obtain and review outlines of their presentations.

▶ Help prepare the agenda and make it decision-oriented. (See sample 7.1)

▶ Create an agenda-based template for minute taking. (See sample 7.2)

▶ Be available to help members in framing motions or resolutions that will facilitate progress at the meeting, and circulate such proposals with the notice of the meeting.

▶ Be available to help members organize reports and documents and ensure that motions and decision-making options are clearly highlighted. A report may be structured as follows:

- The subject of the report
- The mandate of the group or the individual reporting
- Research and analysis done on the designated issues
- Findings and conclusions
- Recommendations and proposed motions

▶ Send the notice of the meeting (in print and/or electronically), including:

- Meeting date, time and place (If needed, give directions to the location)
- Names and titles of those invited to the meeting
- Meeting agenda
- Reports and documents related to the meeting

▶ Get to know names of members. It may be useful to prepare name cards, to be placed in front of them, with their names in large print on both sides.

▶ Contact members to confirm attendance and check the status of follow up items.

▶ Prepare extra copies of the agenda, minutes, relevant reports and documents.

Pre-Meeting Activities

▶ Arrive at least 15 to 30 minutes ahead of time.

▶ If possible, select a seat close to the Chair, or in a place from which you can see and hear as many people as possible.

▶ Ensure there is enough notepaper for recording the minutes (if a laptop computer is not used) and for members who will write motions.

▶ Speak to key meeting participants and find out if there is anything to be aware of, such as a change in a proposed motion, or an emerging new proposal.

▶ Communicate any concerns to the Chair before the meeting begins, find out if he or she has any requests, and provide a list of members who will be late or absent.

▶ Possibly tape record the meeting for backup purposes. If the entire meeting is taped, note tape positions at significant moments, e.g.: when motions are stated, for easy tracking later. Instead of taping the entire meeting, consider taping only summaries, decisions, actions and motions. The group should be advised that the meeting is being taped for minute taking purposes. If freedom of information (FOI) legislation applies, the cassettes may be subject to access requests as long as they exist.

Activities At a Meeting

▶ Use an agenda-based template (see sample 7.2) to capture key discussion points, decisions, and any follow-up actions that were agreed to.

▶ Listen carefully and shift the focus from words to key concepts and ideas.

▶ Convert discussions into concise, objective summaries (see Chapter 2, Sample 2.1).

▶ If unsure of a summary or the wording of a motion, ask permission to read it aloud for confirmation and possible correction. If it is not the group's norm to allow the minute taker to speak up at a meeting, the Chair could read the summary or motion and confirm accuracy with the group.

- ▶ Ask for help if you have any trouble recording the minutes (see Sample 7.3).

- ▶ Keep a neutral demeanor throughout the meeting (facial expressions and body language). This is especially important during public and formal meetings.

- ▶ Keep a list of technical questions to ask certain people after the meeting. This will minimize the need to interrupt and ask for clarifications during the meeting.

Post-Meeting Activities

- ▶ Check with key individuals about unclear or confusing technical terminology.

- ▶ Edit the agenda-based template to create draft minutes. Highlight decisions made and follow-up items that the group agreed on. Consolidate details relating to the same agenda item together, even if the discussion was interrupted midstream.

- ▶ It is common practice to have the Chair review the draft minutes before circulation to members. The Chair may enhance the clarity and accuracy of the minutes, but may not alter the draft minutes to modify decisions with which she or he disagrees.

- ▶ As an option, circulate a draft of the minutes to members for informal feedback. Make only valid changes. If a member tries to impose questionable changes, advise the individual to bring the changes to the next meeting for the group to decide.

- ▶ Add agenda items that were not concluded to the next meeting agenda. For example: if an agenda item was postponed (due to a lack of time), it should be scheduled at the next meeting under *unfinished business*.

- ▶ If needed, prepare a task table (separate from the minutes). The Chair (or the minute taker) can use it to check whether members completed follow-up duties that were assigned to them.

Sample 7.1: Meeting Agenda

Monthly Meeting Agenda
IT Committee of XYZ College

Place:	Committee Room 5
Date:	January 15, 2005
Timing:	2:00 to 4:30 p.m.
Invited:	Derek Lee (facilitator), Information Systems Division
	Monica Rothberg, Accounting Division
	Fred Ferguson, Customer Services Division
	Rebecca Stein, Marketing Division
	Theresa Green, Human Resources Division

Item & Timing	Description & Backup Documents	Responsibility
1. Opening remarks 2:00 to 2:10 p.m.	Chair and members to report on activities	All
2. IT training options 2:10 to 3:20	Bids by three firms to be presented Document REP-IT-100105 (attached)	Derek
	Decision to be made on selecting a firm	All
Break (3:20-3:30)		
3. IT Trends 3:30 to 4:20	Monica Rothberg to report on IT conference Document REP-IT-171204 (attached)	Monica
	Discussion to follow	All
4. Closing remarks 4:20 to 4:30 p.m.	Review of progress and future plans	All

Sample 7.2: Minute Taking Template

Below is an example of an agenda-based template for minute taking. You can prepare it before the meeting, and use your laptop computer to edit it at the meeting.

Minutes of Monthly Meeting
Information Technology (IT) Committee of XYZ College

Date:	January 15, 2005
Time:	2:00 p.m.
Place:	Committee Room 5
Attending:	Derek Lee, Information Systems Division (Chair) Monica Rothberg, Accounting Division Fred Ferguson, Customer Services Division Rebecca Stein, Marketing Division Theresa Green, Human Resources Division (taking minutes)
Absent:	(You may need to move names to this list at the meeting)
Agenda:	1. Selecting a company to conduct Information Technology Training 2. Reviewing emerging IT trends

Agenda Item	Discussion & Consensus	Action Items (follow up)
1. Opening remarks	Derek: Monica: Fred: Rebecca: Theresa:	
2. IT Training	Derek outlined bids by three firms (Document REP-IT-100105). Key points emphasized:_____ Discussion summary (key points made): Decisions:	
3. IT Trends	Monica presented a report on a recent IT conference in New Mexico (REP-IT-171204). Key points presented: Discussion summary (key points made): Decisions:	
4. Closing remarks	Progress made: Future plans:	
Next meeting	February 10, 2005	
Closing time		

Sample 7.3: Minute Taker's Interventions

If this happens in a meeting:	You can do or say something like this:
The group does not conclude an agenda item and proceeds to the next.	Interrupt and ask what the decision was (If this is awkward, pass a note to the Chair): "Before we move on, how do you want me to record this motion? When are you planning to vote on it?"
The exact wording of the consensus or the motion is not clear. For example: a member says "*I so move*" and no one knows what was moved.	"I need some help. What exactly is the motion? I am not sure what to record in the minutes." Or: "Before we move on, can I confirm the motion? What I have is _____. Did I capture it correctly?"
Members are bogged down trying to amend a motion and are getting frustrated and confused.	Pass a note to the Chair: "It may be a good idea to take a break and have a few people work out the wording. If you want, I have notes that can help them out."
Everyone talks at the same time. It is difficult to take minutes.	Pass a note to the Chair or speak up: "Can I ask for a favor? I am having trouble recording more than one conversation simultaneously. Would it be out of line to suggest that only one person speak at a time?"
A member requests that his or her comments be recorded in the minutes verbatim, when your group had agreed to have anecdotal minutes.	Explain why you cannot accommodate the request: "I am having a problem here. The minute taking standards that the Board approved do not allow me to record verbatim minutes. With all due respect, I cannot record statements word for word."

About the Author

Eli Mina, M.Sc., CPP, PRP, is a Vancouver (Canada) based management consultant, speaker, executive coach, and Certified Parliamentarian. In business since 1984, Eli assists his clients in managing meetings, building better boards and councils, dealing with disputes and controversies, demystifying the rules of order, and establishing minute taking standards. Eli's clients come from municipal government, school boards, credit unions, regulatory bodies, non-profit organizations, business and industry.

In addition to "*Mina's Guide to Minute Taking*", Eli wrote "*The Business Meetings Sourcebook*" (AMACOM 2002) and other books on meetings, shared decision-making and rules of order. He has a Master's degree in Electrical Engineering, completed a Conflict Resolution Certificate Program, and holds the designations of a Certified Professional Parliamentarian (CPP) and Professional Registered Parliamentarian (PRP).

Contact information for speaking engagements and consulting assignments:

Phone: 604-730-0377
E-mail: eli@elimina.com
Web site: www.elimina.com

For book ordering information visit www.elimina.com